PERSPECTIVES ON BEHAVIOUR

A Practical Guide to Effective Interventions for Teachers

HARRY AYERS
DON CLARKE
ANNE MURRAY

David Fulton Publishers

London

David Fulton Publishers Ltd
2 Barbon Close, London WC1N 3JX

First published in Great Britain by
David Fulton Publishers Ltd 1995

British Library Cataloguing in Publication Data

A catalogue record for this book is available from the British Library

ISBN 1-85346-364-7

Typeset by Don Clarke
Printed in Great Britain by Bell and Bain Ltd, Glasgow.

Contents

1 Preface 5

2 Introduction 7

3 The Behavioural Perspective 12

4 The Cognitive-behavioural Perspective 34

5 The Ecosystemic Perspective 48

6 The Psychodynamic Perspective 62

7 Using Charts and Books effectively 92

8 Bibliography 100

9 Resources 104

Cognitive Assessment Pupil Questionnaire

Interview Sheet for Carers

Analysis of Interactions Sheet

Pupil Self-control Monitoring Form

Acknowledgements

This book is based on the "Perspectives on Behaviour" course which is an accredited module of the Advanced Diploma in Special Educational Needs, of the University of London Institute of Education. This was an outreach course run by members of the Tower Hamlets Support for Learning Service.

Special acknowledgements to Brahm Norwich (Responsible Tutor for the accredited module at the University of London Institute of Education).

We are indebted to the course participants and teachers in the London Borough of Tower Hamlets for their contributions, time and encouragement. We also thank pupils of schools in Tower Hamlets for their illustrations.

We must also thank the following speakers on the course: Paul Cooper (University of Oxford Department of Education), Brahm Norwich (University of London Institute of Education), Heather Geddes (member of the Forum for the Advancement of Educational Therapy and Therapeutic Teaching – F.A.E.T.T.)

The course was delivered by:

Harry Ayers, Don Clarke, Anne Murray (members of the Tower Hamlets Support for Learning Service) and Brahm Norwich.

Thanks to Heather Geddes (F.A.E.T.T.) and Gill Salmon (F.A.E.T.T.) for their help. Thanks also to Liz Saunders (F.A.E.T.T.) for the term 'puzzling children'.

Also, acknowledgement to Martin Bonathan (SEN Policy Advisor, Birmingham LEA) who as previous Head of Service Development at the Tower Hamlets Support for Learning Service, negotiated the original course module.

We would also like to express our thanks to Liz Vickerie (Director) and Specialist Teachers of the Tower Hamlets Support for Learning Service for their contributions and encouragement.

Created on *Acorn 'A' series* computers
Materials designed using *Acorn DRAW* and *ArtWorks* from *Computer Concepts, TableMate* from *Dalriada Data* and *Poster* from *4Mation*
DeskTop Published using *Impression Publisher* from *Computer Concepts*

Preface

Behaviour – General issues

It is useful to keep in mind a number of general points or issues relating to the concepts of behaviour and behaviour problems.

- Different terms are often used to refer to unacceptable forms of behaviour e.g. **abnormal, maladaptive, anti-social** and **conduct disorder**.

- Debates and indeed controversies have arisen over:

  How far behaviour problems are **relative** to a given **context, culture, society** or **historical period.**

  Whether behaviour problems can be viewed as lying along a **continuum** or are distinct and separate **categories** – a difference of degree or a difference of kind.

  How far behaviour problems reflect an individual's particular **traits** or result from their responses to specific **situations** or are an outcome of **interactions** between traits and situations.

  How far there is a **biological basis** for behaviour problems.

  How far behaviour problems are determined or influenced by **heredity** and / or the **environment**.

  The **extent** or **incidence** of behaviour problems e.g. in connection with **gender** and **ethnic minorities.**

  Ethical issues that relate to changing behaviour.

Even though the issues are not discussed here it is important for the reader to be aware of them.

Why use this book?

This book is a practical guide to four perspectives on BEHAVIOUR.

The four perspectives are:

THE BEHAVIOURAL (or Behaviourist) Focuses on overt, observable and measurable behaviours and their reinforcement in accounting for behaviour.

THE COGNITIVE (or Cognitive-behavioural) Focuses on cognitive processes (beliefs, attitudes, expectations and attributions) in accounting for behaviour. Combines both the cognitive and the behavioural perspective.

THE ECOSYSTEMIC Focuses on positive and negative interactions between systems within the school and those externally that affect the school. These interactions are seen as accounting for behaviour.

THE PSYCHODYNAMIC Focuses on unconscious conflicts arising in early childhood as accounting for current behaviour.

The **aim** of the book is to enable the reader to develop a **structured** approach to emotional and behavioural problems by drawing on one or more of the above perspectives.

It is helpful to plan interventions through a **FIVE-STAGE MODEL**:

- **IDENTIFICATION** of the pupil as a cause for concern
- **ASSESSMENT** of the pupil's problem or WHAT it is
- **FORMULATION** of the pupil's problem or WHY it happens
- **INTERVENTION** or WAYS of dealing with the problem
- **EVALUATION** of the intervention

The above model is a **general schema** which applies to the Behavioural, Cognitive and Ecosystemic perspectives.

In terms of the schema in the fullest sense the Psychodynamic perspective requires a specialised training which most readers may not possess. However, an understanding of the Psychodynamic approach will enable the reader to reflect on how students' behaviour can be affected by unconscious processes and to modify their own classroom practice in accordance with some of the broader ideas.

Introduction

A GENERAL SCHEMA

For BEHAVIOURAL, COGNITIVE, ECOSYSTEMIC and PSYCHODYNAMIC PERSPECTIVES

A GENERAL SCHEMA is a guide which enables teachers to proceed in a structured way in dealing with behaviour problems regardless of the chosen approach or perspective.

It can take the following form:

1 ASSESSMENT **2 FORMULATION**

3 INTERVENTION **4 EVALUATION**

ASSESSMENT PHASE

Describing the pupil's problem

BEHAVIOURAL Assessment techniques: direct observation using event sampling and frequency counts; conducting interviews, using questionnaires, rating scales, checklists and an ABC or functional analysis.

COGNITIVE Assessment techniques: using interviews to explore beliefs, attitudes and attributions; using self-monitoring e.g. keeping a log or diary: using self-rating scales, time-event charts, self-report questionnaires; using an ABC analysis that includes beliefs as well as antecedents, behaviours and consequences.

ECOSYSTEMIC Assessment techniques: data collection i.e. interviews, questionnaires and surveys, on the attitudes, expectations and interactions between teachers, pupils and significant others, and on aspects of the pupil's total environment; sociometry(a method of investigating the relationships between pupils); and the use of systematic observation, checklists and rating scales.

PSYCHODYNAMIC Assessment techniques: using free association, using projective methods eg the Rorschach or inkblot test, the Thematic Apperception Test (TAT) or story-telling tests; using interviews.

FORMULATION PHASE

Why are the pupil's behaviour problems occurring?

BEHAVIOURAL This perspective formulates in terms of the ways in which behaviour problems are being maintained by positive and negative reinforcement.

COGNITIVE This perspective formulates in terms of the ways in which patterns of thought, beliefs, attitudes and attributions are associated with behaviour problems.

ECOSYSTEMIC This perspective formulates in terms of the ways in which behaviour problems result from interactions between the teacher, the pupil and elements of the pupil's total environment. A behaviour problem is not seen as solely located within the pupil but rather as a product of interactions between teachers, pupils and the pupils' environment.

PSYCHODYNAMIC The psychodynamic perspective formulates in terms of a pupil's unconscious preoccupation with their emotional distress stemming from early development and experience. This emerges in the form of emotional and behavioural difficulties.

INTERVENTION PHASE

Methods of changing behaviour

BEHAVIOURAL Interventions are based on operant learning principles e.g. using positive and negative reinforcement, shaping, contingency contracting, token economy and time-out.

COGNITIVE Interventions are based on the premiss that the pupil lacks verbal mediation strategies for developing reflective self-control e.g. problem-solving training, self-instructional training and attribution retraining which can be delivered through modelling, role play and behavioural contingencies (examples being self-rewarding, positive self-statements and rewards for accurate self-evaluation).

ECOSYSTEMIC Interventions are based on the idea of changing the pupil, the pupil's environment and attitudes and expectations through using behavioural, cognitive or psychodynamic techniques as long as the focus is on elements of the entire system. This means that the school setting as well as the pupil has to be considered e.g. the pupil may be taught new behaviours, negative aspects of the school environments should be reduced or eliminated, positive aspects accentuated and teachers' attitudes and expectations should be modified.

PERSPECTIVE SCHEMA	BEHAVIOURAL	COGNITIVE	ECO-SYSTEMIC	PSYCHODYNAMIC
Theoretical basis:	Classical / operant conditioning	Attribution / perceived self-efficacy	Systems / subsystems / Family therapy	Unconscious processes influence conscious behaviour.
Model of person	Behaviour results from learning	Behaviour mediated through cognitive processes	Behaviour is the product of interactions	Behavour is determined by unconscious conflicts
Assessment basis:	Overt, observable, measurable behaviour	Thoughts, beliefs, perceptions, attributions	Interaction within and between systems and subsystems	Ego defences; elements of unconscious phantasy; internal working models
Assessment procedure:	Observation schedules, checklists, rating scales, profiles and ABC	Self-monitoring logs, self-reports, diaries and ABC	Interviews and observation	Projective techniques, interviews
Formulation basis:	Reinforcement and maintaining of problem behaviour by the total environment	Thinking processes mediate problem behaviours	Negative interactions result in self-perpetuating cycles	Unconscious conflicts manifest themselves in emotional difficulties
Formulation:	Problem behaviour caused by maladaptive learning	Problem behaviour caused by maladaptive thinking	Problem behaviour results from negative interactions	Problem behaviour caused by unconscious conflicts
Intervention basis:	Changing overt, observable, measurable behaviour	Changing maladaptive thinking processes	Facilitating positive interactions	Facilitating insight. Strengthening the Ego
Intervention strategies:	Reinforcement programmes, time-out, response costs, contracts, charts, token economy	Problem-solving, self-regulation, attribution retraining	Using techniques of reframing, sleuthing, symptom prescription, positive connotation of function and motive	Interpretation of resistances and defences / unconscious phantasy through transference relationship.
Evaluation basis:	Changes in overt, observable processes	Changes in cognitive processes	Changes in interactions	Insight into unconscious conflicts. Ego strength
Evaluation:	Comparison of behavioural change with baseline	Reattribution, greater self-regulation and problem-solving	New cycle of positive interactions	Increased insight and Ego strength

COMPARISON OF THE FOUR PERSPECTIVES

Some specific ecosystemic programmes are: psycho-educational where teachers develop their awareness of a pupil's total environment and act as 're-educators' of the pupil and significant others in the pupil's environment; setting up parent-teacher partnerships and redesigning the classroom to meet the psychological needs of pupils.

PSYCHODYNAMIC Psychodynamic interventions use methods of varying intensity and directness aimed at resolving or reducing unconscious preoccupations or anxieties which interfere with the pupil's appropriate engagement in the learning situation. When successful, the emotional energy or attention hitherto tied up by the unconscious preoccupations or anxiety is released and the pupil is enabled to direct this towards making progress in learning.

EVALUATION PHASE

Did the intervention produce a change in behaviour?

BEHAVIOURAL Evaluation is based on observation of a pupil's specific target behaviours over the period of the intervention. A pre-intervention baseline (of the pupil's typical behaviour) is established to enable a comparison to made with the pupil's subsequent behaviour after the intervention has been introduced. Other experimental designs e.g. reversal and multiple baseline designs can be used to test whether a change in the pupil's behaviour is the result of the intervention or some other influence. Teachers' and parents' perceptions can also be ascertained.

COGNITIVE Evaluation is based on changes that have occurred in the pupil's beliefs, attitudes and attributions that are associated with a change in the pupil's behaviour. These cognitive changes can be evaluated through the use of self-reports, interviews with teachers, parents and pupils and direct observation of behaviour (as above).

ECOSYSTEMIC Evaluation in part depends on the specific perspective and the type of intervention resulting from that perspective. Given that the purpose of an ecosystemic intervention is to effect a match between the pupil and aspects of his or her environment then a variety of approaches to evaluation need to be considered: e.g. observation, self-reports, interviews, surveys and questionnaires.

PSYCHODYNAMIC Evaluation is based on inferences made by therapists or counsellors as to changes in a pupil's behaviour. In addition use is made of projective methods for the same purpose. NB: Experimental designs have been also been used to evaluate psychotherapy but it is difficult to test.

Don Clarke

Monitoring Book

Form 8 Ha

St Nic

Example of a Behaviour Monitoring Book

Day Date

Period Subject

Don is trying to achieve the following goals. How did he do?

Listening to the teacher

Very well / OK / Not very well

Being pleasant to other pupils

Very well / OK / Not very well

Sitting in his seat

Very well / OK / Not very well

Positive Comments:

Teacher's signature:

The Behavioural Perspective

THE BEHAVIOURAL MODEL

This perspective is based on **Learning Theory** i.e. on **Classical Conditioning Theory** developed by I. PAVLOV and **Operant Conditioning Theory** developed by B. SKINNER. The essential idea is that behavioural and emotional problems arise through maladaptive learning and that they can be resolved through **learning** appropriate responses or **unlearning** inappropriate responses.

It is **behaviourist** because the emphasis is on behaviour that is **overt, observable** and **measurable** and there is no reference to cognitive or unconscious processes. The focus is on current factors that precipitate and maintain behaviour.

CLASSICAL CONDITIONING

Is based on the idea of **conditioned associations** between **stimuli** and **responses**.

This is illustrated by Pavlov's example:

- A **conditioned stimulus** elicits an **unconditioned response**
  For example: a ringing bell elicits attention.
- An **unconditioned stimulus** elicits an un**conditioned response**
  For example: food is continually presented after bell is rung and elicits salivation
- Finally the **conditioned stimulus** elicits the **conditioned response**
  For example: the bell soon elicits salivation on its own.

OPERANT CONDITIONING

This form of conditioning occurs where behaviour is modified or controlled through the manipulation of environmental factors. This is sometimes referred to as **behaviour modification**.

It is where:

An **operant response** occurs and is followed by a **reinforcing stimulus** which increases the likelihood of the response happening again. (For example: a pupil puts her hand up (rather than shouts out and as a consequence the teacher praises her). Responses that are reinforced are likely to recur. A **reinforcer** is simply any event that is observed to increase the likelihood of a response. This form of learning consists of:

- learning **when** to make a response - to **discriminate** between stimuli in terms of those which result in reinforcement when a particular response is forthcoming. (**Discriminative stimuli** tell the pupil **when** responses will or will not result in rewards.)

- learning **what type** of response is required for
- learning **what type** of response must occur in order that reinforcement or rewards follow it. This learning involves **behavioural contingencies** and **reinforcement schedules**. The pupil needs to know what kind of responses are connected to what rewards (the contingencies) and the timing and patterning of rewards (the schedules).

ASSESSMENT

THE RATIONALE

Behavioural assessment is necessary for two reasons:

- In order to find out the **frequency** or how often the problem behaviour takes place. This is necessary so as to determine a **baseline** assessment of the problem behaviour before an intervention is introduced.
- During the intervention it is necessary to establish if the problem behaviour is being reduced or eliminated by reference to the **pre-intervention** baseline.

Behavioural assessment tries to avoid subjectivity where for example teachers' and parents' judgments may not correspond to what is actually occurring. Direct **observation** is used to try and find out the extent of the problem behaviour and the amount of behaviour change.

It must be remembered that observation has its own problems in terms of potential **bias** and recording errors.

A **functional assessment** is a means of behavioural analysis which attempts to relate events occurring before and after the problem behaviours.

MAIN PRINCIPLES

- Behavioural assessment involves initially, identifying overt, **observable** and **specific** behaviours e.g. a pupil's speech acts, wandering around, interfering with others, that are perceived by teachers as problematic.
- Both **excesses** and **deficits** in behaviour are identified along with their appropriateness or inappropriateness e.g. the pupil spends too much time talking about off-task matters and very little time talking about on-task matters.
- Emphasis is placed on **current** patterns of behaviour rather than searching for causes in the distant past e.g. the pupil's existing problem of off-task chatter and how it is being **maintained**. There is a focus on factors that serve to maintain the behaviours e.g. other pupil's joining in and paying attention to the pupil's jokes. When looking at the recent past, consideration is paid to the pupil's learning history i.e. how their behaviour has been **reinforced** e.g. the pupil has gained and enjoyed the attention of other pupils over a long period of time.
- Behavioural **functional analysis** concentrates on the context of the pupil's problem behaviour e.g. if it is in the classroom and in most subjects; the time it occurs e.g. particularly in the afternoons; what happens to the pupil just before it occurs e.g. other pupils crowd around his table; the reaction that occurs around the pupil e.g. other pupils listen intently and what happens after the problem behaviour has taken place e.g. other pupils start laughing.
- Behavioural Assessment avoids using pre-determined labels to describe people with problem behaviours.
- The main aim is to arrive at a clear and specific assessment of the problem by producing a **formulation** of the problem i.e. how it has developed and how it is maintained.

A formulation should lead to a testable hypothesis resulting in interventions with short and long-term **goals**. These goals should be:

***S*PECIFIC**

***M*EASURABLE**

***A*CHIEVABLE**

***R*ELEVANT**

***T*IME-LIMITED**

THE STRATEGIES USED IN BEHAVIOURAL ASSESSMENTS

Behaviours are assessed on the number of discrete problem behaviours occurring or on the length of time that the problem behaviour occurs.

- **FREQUENCY** refers to the number of times the problem behaviour occurs in a particular period of time e.g. the number of times a pupil hits another pupil.
  It is simple to record, only requires a counting measure e.g. a stopwatch, and relates to the goals of most interventions which is to increase or reduce the frequency of a specific problem behaviour.

- **INTERVAL RECORDING** refers to measuring problem behaviour by recording that behaviour during a particular block of time which is itself divided into a number of short intervals e.g. 15 seconds.
  During the interval the problem behaviour (e.g. out-of-seat behaviour) is recorded as having occurred or not occurred e.g. a pupil may be observed for 15 second intervals over a period of 20 minutes. The observer records if the pupil stays in or leaves her seat for the given interval. Interval scoring requires the use of a sheet on which intervals are marked (See '*Assessing Individual Needs*' for a **Fixed Interval Sampling Sheet**). This approach enables an observer to record nearly all kinds of behaviour and the results can be worked out as a percentage.

- **DURATION** is a measure of how long a problem behaviour was performed by a pupil.

- **LATENCY** refers to the length of time it takes before a pupil begins to perform a particular behaviour.

FIXED INTERVAL SAMPLING

Date: 30/

Pupil: Tony | Class: 7 DC | No. in class: 29 | Observer:

Activity: PHSE | Class Behaviour Rating -2 -1 0 +1 +2 | Setting: Form Room

00	15	30	45	00	15	30	45	00	15	30	45	00	15	30	45	00	15	30	45	(1) On Task	(2) Talking	(3) Looking	(4) Physical	(5) Movement	(6) Fidgeting	(7) Noi
1	1	1	1	1	1	3	3	1	3	3	3	1	1	1	3	2	2	1	3	10	2	7				
3	3	1	3	2 1	2 1	2	2 1	3	2	1	3	2 1	2 1	1 T	1 T	1 T	1	1	1	10½	4½	5	Teacher		3.	
1	1	3	1	3	2	2	2 1	1	2	2	2 T	1	1	1	2	1	2	2	2 T	8½	9½	2	Teacher		2	

METHODS OF ASSESSMENT

DIRECT OBSERVATION

Functional analysis is based on observation. Teachers can keep records of a pupil's problem behaviours and any antecedents and consequences of those behaviours.

These reports can be collated and summarised to arrive at conclusions as to the occurrence or non-occurrence of the pupil's problem behaviours at certain times or during certain activities.

These summaries should lead to hypotheses as to the interventions that might modify the problem behaviour.

In observing pupils, teachers should use **behaviour frequency** and **interval recording sheets**.

Issues concerning observation

Ideally, because of the variability of behaviour, a **representative sample** of behaviour should be obtained over an extended period, say two or three weeks

However, the pupil's problem behaviour may be known to occur at particular times or in certain contexts so allowing economical observation.

Observation can be undertaken through using **frequency**, **interval**, **duration** or **latency** methods to record problem behaviour.

Quite often a pupil becomes aware that he or she is being observed and the observer's presence changes the pupil's behaviour (known as **reactivity**). However, this is usually temporary and can be eliminated by the observer being in the context frequently.

It can be useful to have several observers present who have been trained to observe the pupil using the same definition of problem behaviour as this can act as a check on the **reliability** of assessment. Agreement is necessary to avoid the problem of **bias** i.e. seeing improvement or deterioration in the problem behaviour where there is none.

ASSESSMENT INSTRUMENTS

Teachers can make use of the checklists and profiles that enable them to record specific information about the pupil's behaviour in a structured, comprehensive and systematic way.

The **ASSESSMENT PROFILE** are useful in this respect.

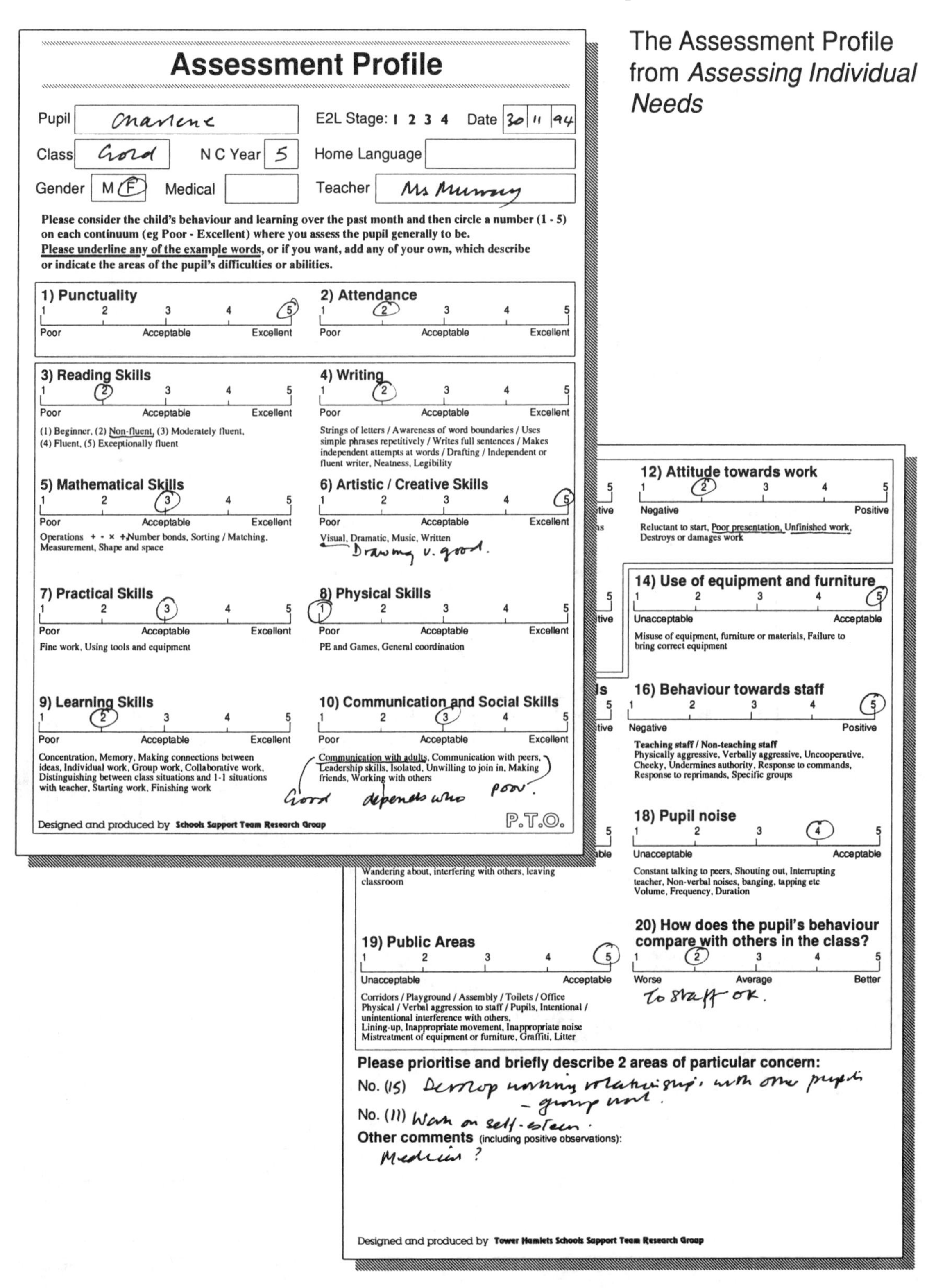

Assessment Profile

Pupil | E2L Stage: 1 2 3 4 | Date
Class | N C Year | Home Language
Gender M F | Medical | Teacher

Please consider the child's behaviour and learning over the past month and then circle a number (1 - 5) on each continuum (eg Poor - Excellent) where you assess the pupil generally to be.
Please underline any of the example words, or if you want, add any of your own, which describe or indicate the areas of the pupil's difficulties or abilities.

1) Punctuality — 1 2 3 4 5 — Poor / Acceptable / Excellent

2) Attendance — 1 2 3 4 5 — Poor / Acceptable / Excellent

3) Reading Skills — 1 2 3 4 5 — Poor / Acceptable / Excellent
(1) Beginner, (2) Non-fluent, (3) Moderately fluent, (4) Fluent, (5) Exceptionally fluent

4) Writing — 1 2 3 4 5 — Poor / Acceptable / Excellent
Strings of letters / Awareness of word boundaries / Uses simple phrases repetitively / Writes full sentences / Makes independent attempts at words / Drafting / Independent or fluent writer, Neatness, Legibility

5) Mathematical Skills — 1 2 3 4 5 — Poor / Acceptable / Excellent
Operations + - × ÷ Number bonds, Sorting / Matching, Measurement, Shape and space

6) Artistic / Creative Skills — 1 2 3 4 5 — Poor / Acceptable / Excellent
Visual, Dramatic, Music, Written

7) Practical Skills — 1 2 3 4 5 — Poor / Acceptable / Excellent
Fine work, Using tools and equipment

8) Physical Skills — 1 2 3 4 5 — Poor / Acceptable / Excellent
PE and Games, General coordination

9) Learning Skills — 1 2 3 4 5 — Poor / Acceptable / Excellent
Concentration, Memory, Making connections between ideas, Individual work, Group work, Collaborative work, Distinguishing between class situations and 1-1 situations with teacher, Starting work, Finishing work

10) Communication and Social Skills — 1 2 3 4 5 — Poor / Acceptable / Excellent
Communication with adults, Communication with peers, Leadership skills, Isolated, Unwilling to join in, Making friends, Working with others

Designed and produced by Schools Support Team Research Group

P.T.O.

12) Attitude towards work — 1 2 3 4 5 — Negative / Positive
Reluctant to start, Poor presentation, Unfinished work, Destroys or damages work

14) Use of equipment and furniture — 1 2 3 4 5 — Unacceptable / Acceptable
Misuse of equipment, furniture or materials, Failure to bring correct equipment

16) Behaviour towards staff — 1 2 3 4 5 — Negative / Positive
Teaching staff / Non-teaching staff
Physically aggressive, Verbally aggressive, Uncooperative, Cheeky, Undermines authority, Response to commands, Response to reprimands, Specific groups

Wandering about, interfering with others, leaving classroom

18) Pupil noise — 1 2 3 4 5 — Unacceptable / Acceptable
Constant talking to peers, Shouting out, Interrupting teacher, Non-verbal noises, banging, tapping etc
Volume, Frequency, Duration

19) Public Areas — 1 2 3 4 5 — Unacceptable / Acceptable
Corridors / Playground / Assembly / Toilets / Office
Physical / Verbal aggression to staff / Pupils, Intentional / unintentional interference with others,
Lining-up, Inappropriate movement, Inappropriate noise
Mistreatment of equipment or furniture, Graffiti, Litter

20) How does the pupil's behaviour compare with others in the class? — 1 2 3 4 5 — Worse / Average / Better

Please prioritise and briefly describe 2 areas of particular concern:
No.
No.
Other comments (including positive observations):

Designed and produced by Tower Hamlets Schools Support Team Research Group

The Assessment Profile from *Assessing Individual Needs*

Primary Assessment Profile Score

Pupil Charlene Class Gold E2L Stag

Date 30.11.94

1) Punctuality	1	2								
2) Attendance	1	2								
3) Reading Skills	1	2								
4) Writing	1	2								
5) Mathematical Skills	1	2								
6) Artistic / Creative Skills	1	2								
7) Practical Skills	1	2	(3)	4	5	1	2	3	4	5
8) Physical Skills	(1)	2	3	4	5	1	2	3	4	5
9) Learning Skills	1	(2)	3	4	5	1	2	3	4	5
10) Communication and Social Skills	1	2	(3)	4	5	1	2	3	4	5
11) Attitude towards self	(1)	2	3	4	5	1	2	3	4	5
12) Attitude towards work	1	(2)	3	4	5	1	2	3	4	5
13) Attitude towards school	1	2	(3)	4	5	1	2	3	4	5
14) Use of equipment and furniture	1	2	3	4	(5)	1	2	3	4	5
15) Behaviour towards other pupils	(1)	2	3	4	5	1	2	3	4	5
16) B										

The Primary Score Sheet allows a class teacher or SENCO to collate three different sets results thus making comparisons over time easy.

Secondary Assessment Profile Score She

Sheet no. 1

11.30.94

Jas

	Punctuality 1	Attendance 2	Reading 3	Writing 4	Maths 5	Artistic 6	Practical 7	Physical 8	Learning 9	Social 10	Self 11	Work 12
MATHS	5	5	5	4	5				4	3	5	4
ENGLISH	5	5	2	2		3	3		2	2	3	2
SCIENCE	5	5	3	3	3	3	4	3	4	2	2	3
TECHNOLOGY												
GEOGRAPHY	5	5	2	2		5	4	3	4	1	2	2
HISTORY												
ART	4	3	3	3		1	1		2	1	2	1
ES												
C	5	5	3	2	3	4	1	4	5	1	1	1
ES												
E.												

The Secondary Score Sheet allows a Form Tutor or a Head of Year to collate forms from a number of staff and to collate the results in an easy to evaluate format.

BEHAVIOURAL INTERVIEWING

The AIMS of such an interview are to:

- Acquire information about the child's concerns e.g. fears, anxieties, wishes and ideals.
- Determine current reasons why the child maintains the problem behaviours.
- Find out historical factors that contribute to the child's behaviour.
- Identify 'significant others' and events that reinforce the child's behaviour.
- Discuss with the child assessment procedures and possible interventions and their aims.

When interviewing the child the interviewer should:

- Listen to the child's definition and account of the problem.
- Assess the strengths and weaknesses of the child.
- Find out from the child what rewards or sanctions influence their behaviour.

When interviewing the parents/carers the interviewer should:

- Listen to the parents' or carers' definitions and accounts of the child's problems. It is worth being aware that they may not perceive the cause of the problem as within their child.
- Assess how far the parents or carers are able to control or influence their child's behaviour and in what ways this is achieved.

When interviewing teachers the interviewer should:

- Listen to the teachers' definitions and accounts of the child's problems.
- Ask as to the frequency, intensity and duration of the child's behaviour and the contexts in which it occurs.
- Ask teachers to identify the child's strengths and weaknesses.
- Get teachers to state what strategies they are using with the child and what rewards and sanctions have been tried.
- The accumulated information derived from the various interviews will contribute to the total assessment process especially where observation is limited or restricted.

THE ABC MODEL OF BEHAVIOURAL ANALYSIS

This model provides a way of analyzing behaviour

A refers to the antecedent conditions i.e. what precedes the pupil's behaviour.

B refers to the behaviour itself, what the pupil is actually doing in physical terms not what the teacher thinks or infers that the pupil is doing.

C refers to the consequences of the pupil's behaviour, what happens to the pupil and the reactions of others.

ANTECEDENTS	BEHAVIOUR	CONSEQUENCES
Doing individual work in English	*Pokes or touches other pupils*	*They try to avoid him and sometimes hit him back.*
Whilst he is supposed to be working on his own	*Calls other pupils names*	*They call him names back. He then gets very angry.*
In the 'up-front' section of the lesson	*Calls out to teacher*	*Teacher sometimes ignores him. At other times he gets angry and shouts at the pupil.*

A serious example of the ABC analysis

Looking at the elements in more detail:

A: Events prior to a pupil's behaviour may prompt that behaviour. The teacher needs to be aware of occurrences that lead to the pupil's problem behaviour and the consequences of it in terms of other pupils in the class. Antecedents can be **immediate** e.g. the classroom situation or **background** and might include the pupil's self-esteem, family relationships or general attitudes towards school. (See '*Assessing Individual Needs*' for greater detail and photocopiable forms.)

B: Teachers should define the presenting behaviour difficulties clearly and precisely. It is useful to count the frequency of the pupil's behaviours.

C: Consequences are rewarding or punishing, therefore the teacher should find out what aspects of their classroom management and teaching are rewarding pupils appropriately or inappropriately. Teacher approval and praise should be directed to the pupil's behaviours the teacher wishes to encourage. Minor problems should be ignored by the teacher. Punishment should be avoided where it is likely to have counter-productive consequences or be ineffective. Teachers should also be conscious that they might be inadvertently rewarding problem behaviour.

ANTECEDENTS	BEHAVIOUR	CONSEQUENCES
Feels he has to make an impact and change things	*Orders people about and imposes ridiculous demands*	*Smirks and sounds self-righteous – Other people get angry with him*
Other people irritate him or have good ideas which he doesn't like	*Calls them names*	*Tries to defend himself but is made to make amends*
When asked to appear in front of The House	*Does strange things to his hair*	*Gets a lot of attention – people laugh and call him "Bouffant Boy'*

A less serious example of the ABC analysis

BEHAVIOURAL FORMULATION

A **behavioural formulation** should be based on a behavioural assessment and consist of the following:

- A **descriptive statement** of the main problems or difficulties in behavioural terms
- Some **hypothesis** as to what is **causing** or **maintaining** the problems or difficulties
- Some idea as to how these problems or difficulties could be **managed**
- Some idea as to the likely **outcome**

AN EXAMPLE:

John is a 10 year old boy with reading difficulties and who is frequently out of his seat in the classroom (as measured through formal observation - fixed interval sampling).

John when presented with reading work by the teacher leaves his seat and moves around the classroom talking to other pupils who laugh when he talks to them.

Through leaving his seat he avoids reading and this leads him to continue to stay out of his seat so maintaining the problem behaviour.

John needs his reading skills improved through an appropriate reading programme along with paired reading and peer tutoring.

He also needs a positive reinforcement programme that encourages him to stay in his seat and to be on task e.g. a behaviour chart or personalised report book.

If John's reading skills improve and he responds to the reinforcement programme this will hopefully increase his on task behaviour.

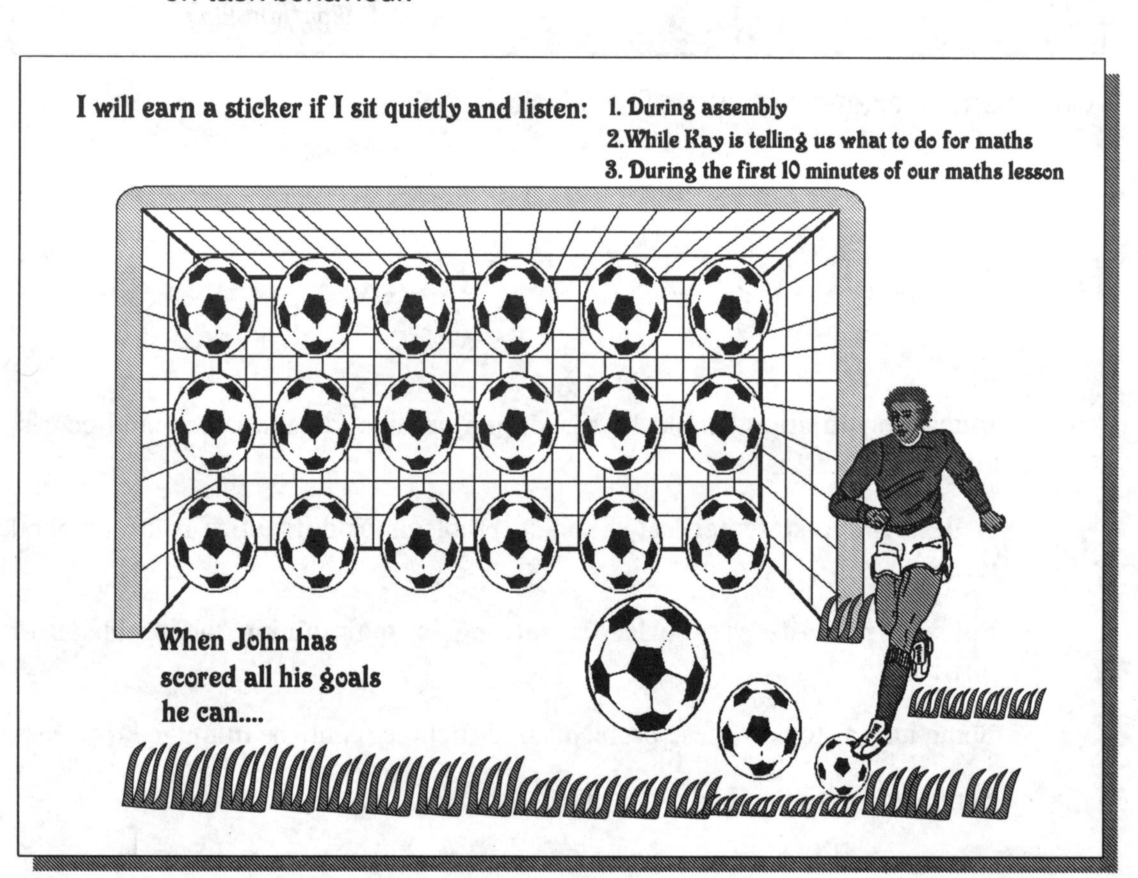

An example of a Behaviour Chart

BEHAVIOURAL INTERVENTION

DEFINITION

A behavioural intervention is a planned, systematic approach to behavioural change based on classical and operant conditioning but also draws on developments in the cognitive and social learning spheres where cognitive-behavioural interventions are undertaken.

THE AIM

The aim of behavioural interventions is to bring about behavioural change or to enable behavioural change to occur i.e. an increase, decrease or extinguishing of behaviours.

FOCUS OF THE INTERVENTION

Individual, group, class or whole school.

THE PROCEDURE

- Decide who the **participants** are, what will they do and under what conditions
- Decide who the **client** is: school, teachers, parents, pupils
- Agree on a limited number of prioritized, **target** behaviours
- Agree on the objectives of the intervention. These should be **Specific**, **Measurable**, **Achievable**, **Relevant** and **Time-limited** (SMART).
- Establish a **baseline** in order to help define the problem and to provide a standard for comparison
- Establish agreed **criteria for success** or **performance indicators**
- Plan how the intervention will be **monitored**
- Plan how the chosen intervention will be **phased** out

If the intervention appears to be failing it may be necessary to consider the following points:

- Is re-assessment indicated?
- Is it necessary to modify or change the intervention?
- Is the client resistant?
- Does the client lack the necessary skills and/or resources to cope with the intervention?
- Is the behavioural approach with the client inappropriate?

TYPES OF INTERVENTIONS

There are basically two types of intervention:

- Those which **increase** particular behaviours through:

  Positive reinforcement

  Negative reinforcement

  Contingency contracting

  Shaping

  Token economy

- Those which **decrease or eliminate** undesirable behaviour through:

  Extinction

  Time out

  Punishment

  Response cost

Positive reinforcement:

Positive reinforcement is the immediate presentation of a stimulus following a desired response that increases the likelihood of that response happening again in the future.

A positive reinforcer describes the reinforcing event itself.

A positive reinforcer cannot be determined in advance. In order to find out whether something is a reinforcer for a particular pupil it is necessary to experiment to see whether a particular behaviour increases as a result of its use.

It should be made clear to the pupil that the acquisition of a positive reinforcer is **contingent** or dependent upon the pupil performing the desired behaviour.

For a positive reinforcer to be effective it should be **given immediately** the desired behaviour is displayed.

Primary reinforcers are biologically based e.g. food and drink. These can be powerful but depend on the pupil being in a state of deprivation which is unlikely.

Secondary reinforcers are preferable to primary reinforcers. Secondary reinforcers include the use of social stimuli e.g. the use of praise, the opportunity to engage in preferred activities and the use of tokens. Their value has been learned and unlike primary reinforcers do not have biological significance.

Reinforcers can also be **affirmative** and **informative** e.g. praise can indicate that a pupil's behaviour is 'fine' (**affirmative**) or 'you have stayed in your seat, well done' (**informative**).

Informative reinforcement is more constructive in that this form of feedback given to the pupil tells him or her specifically what they are praised for.

Negative reinforcement

Negative reinforcement is the removal of an **aversive stimulus** or **negative reinforcer** which results in the target behaviour increasing. In the classroom negative reinforcement occurs where a pupil performs a behaviour and as a result the teacher removes something the pupil dislikes.

An example: a pupil starts to work hard **after** the teacher has said to the pupil that he will not have to do homework if he completes the class work during the day. (The homework, already given, is the aversive stimulus for this pupil.)

Teachers can inadvertently use negative reinforcement e.g. in the case of a pupil complaining about doing classwork, the teacher takes away the work thus the pupil learns that complaining leads to the termination of the aversive stimulus, the classwork and as a result the pupil's complaining increases.

Using negative reinforcement has disadvantages as it might encourage the pupil to engage in escape or avoidance behaviours e.g. a pupil **escaping** by leaving the classroom or by **avoiding** through playing truant.

Positive reinforcement is the recommended intervention rather than negative reinforcement.

Shaping

Shaping is the consistent reinforcement of **successive approximations** to the target behaviour until the target behaviour is achieved. It is used where the level of performance of the behaviour is low.

During the shaping process the teacher reinforces only those responses that approximate to the desired behaviour. The criterion will shift as the pupil gets closer and closer to the target behaviour.

Example: increasing a pupil's in-seat behaviour by reinforcing for each successive increase in time spent in seat i.e. 3, 5, 10 minutes.......

Effective shaping requires that:

- There must be a clear definition of the target behaviour.
- The pupil must be performing the behaviour albeit at a low level and that behaviour must be able to be shaped.
- The intervals must not be too large or too small.
- A decision is made as to how long the pupil remains at the current level before being encouraged to perform at the next stipulated level.

Contingency contracting

A behaviour contract is an agreement between two or more parties that sets down the responsibilities of the parties concerning a particular activity that will lead to the achieving of specific target behaviours.

The use of contingency contracting is based on an idea developed by Premack (1965) which states that that a behaviour performed at a high frequency can be used to increase one having a low frequency or, if you perform x then you will receive y.

The basis of contracting is the idea of individualizing behaviour control so that it responds to the pupil's various needs. The pupil can play an active role in contracting.

The teacher draws up the contract with the pupil and parents stipulating specific target behaviours

For the **effective use** of contracting certain conditions need to be met :

- Reinforcement should be immediate once the target behaviour is performed
- Initial contracts should allow for successive approximations to the target behaviours
- Reinforcement should be frequent and in small amounts
- Contracts should be couched positively in terms of achievement
- The contract should be realistic and fair, asking the pupil to achieve reasonable targets over a reasonable period of time
- The contract must be clear to all the parties so that what it requires is

unambiguous and thus avoids future mistrust

- The contract should be freely accepted by the pupil and not forced on the pupil
- The contract should be reviewed and evaluated

Token economy

A token economy is a reinforcement system in which tokens are earned through a pupil, group or class performing specific target behaviours.

Tokens can take various forms including: points, stars, smiling faces stickers etc. These can then be used as a means of earning particular rewards e.g. preferred activities.

For a token economy to be **effective** certain conditions need to be met:

- The target behaviours must be clear to pupils.
- The rate at which tokens are exchanged for rewards must be specified clearly.
- The level of performance required to earn tokens must be established.
- Emphasis should be on what pupils can achieve and the earning of tokens as a challenge.
- A reward menu should be agreed and drawn up linking numbers of tokens with particular types of rewards.
- Initially a limited system should be implemented.
- Tokens should be awarded immediately.

Extinction

The aim of **extinction** is to withhold or to cease reinforcing a behaviour that has been reinforced e.g. in the case of a pupil who keeps demanding and receiving attention for calling out, the teacher stops paying attention unless the pupil raises their hand.

For this technique to be **effective** it has to be:

- Based on an observable connection between the teacher's attention and the pupil's inappropriate behaviour.
- Used by the teacher consistently and persistently.
- Used along with the employment of positive reinforcement.
- Based on the consideration as to whether the behaviour can be tolerated until it extinguishes.

Time-out

The idea behind **time-out** is to remove a pupil from a situation where the pupil is being reinforced to a setting which is non-reinforcing. A pupil can be put in a time-out either within the classroom or by being excluded from the classroom e.g. by being sent to stand outside the room or by being sent to a special time-out room

For time-out to be **effective** it is necessary to:

- Ensure that the pupil does not find time-out rewarding.
- Make sure that it is applied consistently over a specified period.
- Let the pupil know what rule-infringements will result in time-out.
- Inform the pupil as to how time-out will operate prior to its use in the classroom.

For a time-out **room** or **area** to be **effective** the following conditions should be met:

- The room or area should not reinforce the pupil's behaviour e.g. being able to chat and laugh with other pupils and avoid work.
- The time spent in the room or area should be brief as possible.
- The room or area should be adequately supervised.
- Records should be kept of the pupil's attendance in the room or area and the reason for being sent and should be used to evaluate its effectiveness.

Punishment

The aim of **punishment or the use of sanctions** is to decrease or eliminate a specific behaviour.

There are two types: the use of an **aversive stimulus** as a result of a specific behaviour e.g. a reprimand, detention and writing out lines. Alternatively taking away or **subtracting** from a pupil something they like e.g. a token, this is called **response-cost**.

Punishment in these senses in the short-term is undoubtedly effective but its use over a long period can lead to problems:

- It may simply suppress the pupil's behaviour temporarily.
- It presents a negative way of relating to others for the pupil to model e.g. aggression

- It does not inform the pupil precisely as to which specific behaviours should be performed
- It can lead to the pupil experiencing emotional stress, becoming withdrawn or avoiding the lesson
- It may evoke in the pupil intense dislike of the punisher rather than change in the pupil's behaviour
- What the teacher perceives as punishment may actually be reinforcing for the pupil e.g. being sent out of the class

If **punishment** is used then it is better to implement it in the following ways:

- Specify for which rule-infringements punishment will be used and draw up a graded tariff of punishments
- Display in the classroom a code of conduct
- Apply the punishment consistently and immediately
- Apply the punishment fairly to all offending pupils
- Avoid punishing a group or class for the misbehaviour of an individual or individuals
- Avoid being emotional when punishing pupils
- Use positive reinforcement as well as punishment

With regard to **reprimands** it is better to:

- Use them in relation to specific behaviours
- Avoid using them to be derogatory towards the pupil
- Use them immediately along with loss of privileges
- Avoid sarcasm or embarrassing the pupil in front of others
- Avoid referring to or harping on past incidents
- Try and use non-verbal reprimands along with or instead of verbal reprimand

BEHAVIOUR CONTRACTS

What are they?

Behaviour contracts specify particular behaviours which the parties to a problem would like to be seen performed. The idea is for all the parties to work together towards agreed aims that are specific, realistic, observable and measurable.

How are they designed?

Contracts are specific written agreements about future behaviour that are based on two main ideas:

- There is a definite and unambiguous public commitment to a future action plan which is entered into voluntarily.
- That the parties to it agree on ways of encouraging and maintaining positive behaviour.

Definitions of the behaviours to be encouraged must be accurately defined. The parties must negotiate on identifying the main behaviours that need to be achieved and should agree on what constitutes improved behaviour. Contracts work best where the parties involved have the power to change things for others. It is best to begin with realistic and achievable small steps rather than try and achieve major change in one big leap. The aim is to achieve a 'reasonable' level of behaviour that all can agree on.

How are they negotiated?

- All the parties involved must feel they have a say in its composition
- All the parties must see that they benefit from it
- Contracts should be renegotiable where they are failing

For a **contract** be effective the following conditions should be met:

- The contract should be couched in positive terms and should specify, where possible, rewarding consequences for all the parties involved.
- Once agreed, a draft should be typed as a basis for further discussion. The agreement should be couched in clear and unambiguous language. Each party should have a copy.
- Reviews of the operation of the contract should be agreed in advance.
- The contract can be phased out gradually if it is achieving its aims.

The main function of contracts

- Contracts are not a panacea but can be effective in bringing together the different parties involved with a particular behavioural problem.
- They provide the parties concerned with a structure that enables them to discuss the behaviour problems in a specific way leading to mutually agreed solutions.

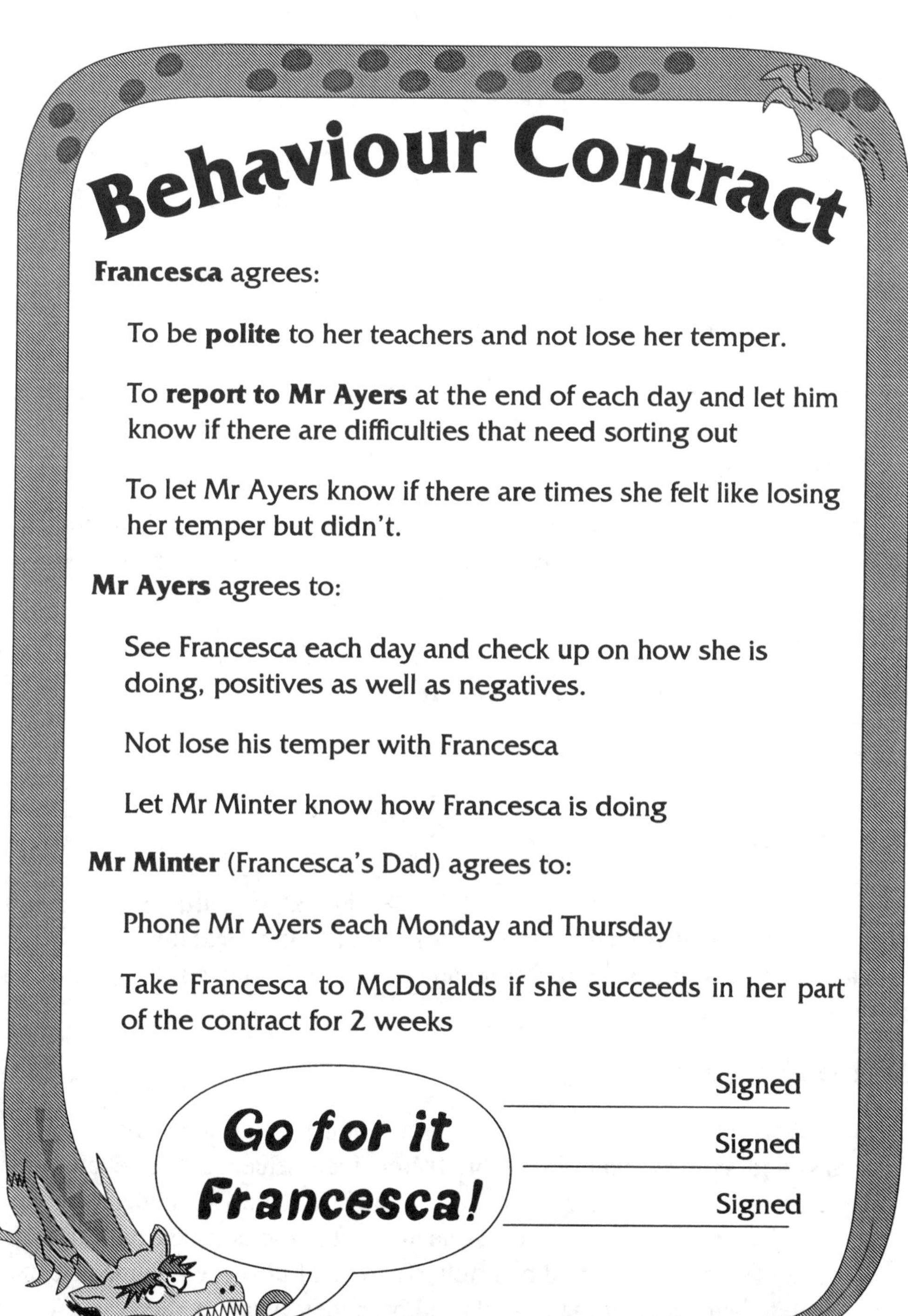

Behaviour Contract

Francesca agrees:

To be **polite** to her teachers and not lose her temper.

To **report to Mr Ayers** at the end of each day and let him know if there are difficulties that need sorting out

To let Mr Ayers know if there are times she felt like losing her temper but didn't.

Mr Ayers agrees to:

See Francesca each day and check up on how she is doing, positives as well as negatives.

Not lose his temper with Francesca

Let Mr Minter know how Francesca is doing

Mr Minter (Francesca's Dad) agrees to:

Phone Mr Ayers each Monday and Thursday

Take Francesca to McDonalds if she succeeds in her part of the contract for 2 weeks

Signed ____________

Signed ____________

Signed ____________

THE BEHAVIOURAL APPROACH TO TEACHING AND LEARNING

This approach advocated by K. Wheldall and F. Merrett (1987) is outlined below:

BASIC ASSUMPTIONS

- It is a structured approach that leads to appropriate practice.
- This approach has been found to be effective empirically in many different institutional, interpersonal and personal contexts.
- Most behaviour is learned within the limits set by genetics and is the result of an interaction between the individual and their environment. Behaviour is shaped through reinforcing events.
- Behaviour is relative to what is considered adaptive or maladaptive in a given social or cultural context.
- Many emotional and behavioural problems are the result of faulty learning or failure to learn i.e. they arise through the processes of classical and operant conditioning.
- Cognitive and unconscious processes are not included in this approach except in the case of the cognitive-behavioural perspective where consideration of cognitive processes is integrated with the behavioural approach.
- This approach is seen as desirable in terms of it being easy to learn, easy to implement and as amenable to empirical evaluation.

TECHNIQUES

This approach refers to the application of **behavioural techniques** to teaching and refers to the theory that behaviour is primarily the result of **learning** but that what is learnt can be changed. Behavioural change can be achieved by controlling the consequences of that behaviour.

The main teaching points are:

- Teachers should direct their attention to their pupils' **observable** behaviour in class and the overt and observable factors that influence that behaviour. This is preferable to speculating about unconscious conflicts or underlying problems that arise during early infancy as such speculation is based on a high level of inference. Teachers should carefully **define** and **observe** the **specific** and overt problem behaviour of their pupils and base their judgments on these definitions and observations.

- Nearly all pupil behaviour is the result of learning. Genetics sets limits but behaviour is still the result of learning within those limits. Positive and negative behaviour can be learned but can also be unlearned. Teachers need to think of strategies that encourage their pupils to learn appropriate behaviour or unlearn inappropriate behaviour.

- Behavioural change needs to be measured. **measurement** enables teachers to be more precise and objective in estimating how far pupils have improved their behaviour. This measurement is achieved through a **frequency** count of the pupil's problem behaviours.

- Pupils learn on the basis of repeating behaviours that have been **reinforced** or rewarded. The emphasis should be on the teacher rewarding pupils for positive behaviour and setting up situations which pupils find rewarding or where they can be rewarded. There is evidence supporting the idea that rewarding positive behaviour is more effective than punishment.

- Behaviour is also influenced by its **context** or **environment** therefore it is necessary for the teacher to consider the effects of their classroom environment on their pupils‘ behaviour in terms of reinforcement. The context not only refers to the classroom itself but also aspects like seating or grouping arrangements.

BEHAVIOURAL EVALUATION

This type of evaluation is dependent on establishing a **pre-intervention baseline** which means determining systematically the frequency and duration of the observable target behaviours of an identified pupil over a number of weeks. This is achieved by using appropriate observation schedules. This baseline will be a benchmark for comparing the frequency and duration of the target behaviours after an intervention.

By making comparisons between the pre-intervention baseline and the end point of the intervention it should be possible to evaluate the intervention through observing that the target behaviours have either increased or decreased or that no change has occurred. This can provide an objective account of changes in a pupil's behaviour given the caveats of observer reactivity and bias. This structured approach is to be contrasted with the subjectivity of a teacher's perceptions based on erratic and intermittent observation of a pupil's behaviours.

The Cognitive-Behavioural Perspective

For brevity, we will refer to the cognitive-behavioural perspective as the **cognitive perspective**.

THE COGNITIVE MODEL

The cognitive perspective on behaviour is based on three fundamental tenets:

- Cognitive processes can bring about changes in behaviour.
- Cognitive processes can be monitored and changed.
- Behavioural change can be elicited through changes in cognition.

COGNITIVE PROCESSES include:

PERCEPTIONS	**ATTITUDES**	**IMAGES**
EXPECTATIONS	**ATTRIBUTIONS**	**BELIEFS**

Given that these processes lead to certain kinds of behaviour, by altering these processes behavioural change is facilitated. Pupils' perceptions are important in determining how they will react in particular situations. They may react quite differently to the same situation depending on their differing perceptions. Teachers and pupils view other pupils and teachers from different viewpoints and these need to be considered when thinking of how to bring about changes in behaviour.

There are three main categories of cognitive interventions:

- **COPING-SKILLS**
- **PROBLEM-SOLVING SKILLS**
- **COGNITIVE RESTRUCTURING**

COGNITIVE ASSESSMENT

Cognitive assessment is a form of assessment that examines cognitive processes and how they relate or connect to behaviour. It is an attempt to identify the particular thoughts and thinking processes individuals engage in and their consequences for their behaviour. Through identifying those processes behavioural change can be facilitated.

The elements of cognitive assessment include the following techniques:

SELF-REPORT ***OBSERVATION*** ***INTERVIEWS***

BEHAVIOUR RATING SCALES

as well as the following modes of analysis:

SELF-CONCEPT	***TASK PERFORMANCE***
SOCIOMETRIC	***ATTRIBUTIONAL STYLE***

INTERVIEWS

The aim is to arrive at descriptions and definitions of specific problems and concomitant cognitive processes.

Interviews with parents

- Ask about specific behaviours. The use of the **ABC** or **functional analysis** is helpful in this respect.
- Ask about their expectations of the pupil's behaviour
- Ask for their perceptions of the pupil's developmental and behavioural history

Interviews with pupils

- Find out if the pupil is aware of having behaviour difficulties?
- Find out their account of the problems they experience and their attributional style, i.e. whether they blame themselves or others or their environment.
- Find out whether the pupil lacks the social skills for thinking through a problem or for performing the desired behaviour.
- Find out if the pupil has little or no idea of what is expected of them.
- Find out whether the pupil lacks motivation by asking them about rewards for good behaviour and consequences for failing to perform desirable behaviour.

Interviews with teachers

The **COGNITIVE ASSESSMENT PROFILE** in this book can be used to record a pupil's perceptions of their behaviour in class and around the school.

- Find out if the teacher experiences the pupil as a problem
- Find out the teacher's perceptions and expectations of the pupil.
- Find out whether the teacher thinks the pupil lacks particular types of skills e.g. learning, social and communication skills.

BEHAVIOUR RATING SCALES

These scales enable teachers to rate a pupil's behaviour based on the teacher's perceptions. They are useful in providing ratings from a number of teachers and help to raise the awareness of other problem behaviours.

(See the Assessment Profiles in '*Assessing Individual Needs*' in this series).

TASK PERFORMANCE

Watching how a pupil performs on a set task may give clues as to how the pupil is thinking about that task (**metacognition**) and the feelings they have as they engage with the task.

It may give an idea as to how effective they are in terms of problem-solving behaviour and their strategies or the lack of them.

SELF-REPORT

The aim of putting a pupil on self-report is to assess the pupil's expectations, attributions and self-concept.

A pupil's **self-efficacy** can be determined. This is the pupil's expectations of success in terms of performing desirable behaviours.

The pupil can state how they expect to do in relation to specific behaviours.

A pupil's **attributional style** can be assessed. This is how the pupil makes similar attribution of causes across different contexts and times. This means looking at a pupil's

COGNITIVE ASSESSMENT PUPIL QUESTIONNAIRE

This form can be used as a means of assessing a pupil's thoughts, attitudes, expectations and beliefs in the school context.

Circle appropriate number on each continuum and underline or add relevant words

Unless otherwise indicated: 1 = Poor 3 = OK 5 = Excellent

BEHAVIOUR:

What do you THINK about your attitude in:

1) Classrooms 1 2 3 4 5 **2) Corridors** 1 2 3 4 5

3) Assembly 1 2 3 4 5 **4) Toilets** 1 2 3 4 5

5) Playground 1 2 3 4 5 **6) Outside school** 1 2 3 4 5

7) How do you behave? 1 2 3 4 5

Interfering Helpful Unhelpful Rude Polite Violent Friendly Talkative Loud Quiet Hardworking Lazy

8) What do you THINK about changing your behaviour?

1 Unable to change 2 3 Maybe able to change 4 5 Able to change

I don't have the power I do have the power I don't want to I want to

Teachers stop me Teachers will help me Pupils stop me Other pupils will help me

9) What do you think of yourself? 1 2 3 4 5

Confident Lacking in confidence Attractive Unattractive Clever Stupid Interested Disinterested

10) In general, do you THINK teachers' behaviour towards you is:

1 2 3 4 5

Helpful Unhelpful Unfriendly Polite Rude Friendly Caring Aggressive Interested Not interested

In particular?

11) What do you THINK about the behaviour of other pupils towards:

YOURSELF: 1 2 3 4 5 *EACH OTHER:* 1 2 3 4 5 *TEACHERS:* 1 2 3 4 5

12) What do you think of your school? 1 2 3 4 5

Nice building Unpleasant building A friendly place An unfriendly place A safe place

An unsafe place A good number of people Too crowded Too noisy Dirty

Designed by Don Clarke and Harry Ayers at the Support for Learning Service in Tower Hamlets

WORK:

13) What do you THINK about the level of work?

1 = Too difficult 2 = Difficult 3 = Just right 4 = Easy

Mathematics 1 2 3 4 5

English 1 2 3 4 5

Science 1 2 3 4 5

14) What do THINK about the relevance of the work to you

1 = None 2 = Little 3 = Some 4 = A lot 5 = Com

Mathematics 1 2 3 4 5

English 1 2 3 4 5

Science 1 2 3 4 5

15) What do you THINK about your level of achievement?

1 = Poor 2 = Not very good 3 = Average 4 = Good 5 = Very

Mathematics 1 2 3 4 5

English 1 2 3 4 5

Science 1 2 3 4 5

16) Do you THINK you can do better?

1 = Not at all 2 = Possibly 3 = Some 4 = Quite a lot

Mathematics 1 2 3 4 5

English 1 2 3 4 5

Science 1 2 3 4 5

If I tried harder If the work was made more interesting If I received more help If I br

17) What do THINK about your effort?

1 = Poor 2 = Not very good 3 = Average 4 = Good 5 = Very

Mathematics 1 2 3 4 5

English 1 2 3 4 5

Science 1 2 3 4 5

Any other comments?

Designed by Don Clarke and Harry Ayers at the Support for Learning Service in Tower Hamlets

The Cognitive Assessment Pupil Questionnaire.

may have an **Internal** or **External Locus of Control** (Rotter and Hochreich, 1975). It is internal if the pupil sees the cause of their behaviour as originating from within themselves. It is external if they see their behaviour as resulting from outside forces.

There is a greater chance for a pupil to improve their behaviour if they have an internal locus of control.

A pupil's **self-concept** is how a particular pupil thinks and feels about themselves. The goals and the evaluation of an intervention should include reference to the pupil's self-concept as it is an important indication of a successful intervention.

OBSERVATION

Behavioural assessment based on direct observation of pupils is still useful even though the emphasis is predominantly on the assessment of cognitive states and processes. Observation can be undertaken through the use of Fixed Interval Sampling and Behaviour Frequency Recording Sheets. The ABC sheet can be used to provide a **functional analysis** of behaviour.

MATHS Self-Monitoring Sheet

Date [ ] Day [ ]

I brought the right equipment:

A pen *A Ruler*

The text book *Calculator*

How quickly did I settle down?

Not very *Quite* *Very quickly*

How hard did I work?

Not very *Quite* *Very hard*

How hard was the work?

Not very *Quite* *Very hard*

What couldn't I do?

[ ]

In the example below, each segment of a wheel represents 1 minute. Liz colours in a segment for each minute she works on each task. This would be done using a suitable timer.

Day [ ] Date [ ]

Liz is trying hard to work on her own

TASKS:

To [ ]

for [ ] minutes

12 1 2 3 4 5 6 7 8 9 10 11

To [ ]

for [ ] minutes

12 1 2 3 4 5 6 7 8 9 10 11

To [ ]

for [ ] minutes

12 1 2 3 4 5 6 7 8 9 10 11

Today I think I did: **Not very well** **OK** **Very well**

Sarah thinks Liz worked [ ] today

In particular, she [ ]

Two examples of pages from Cognitive Monitoring books

SOCIOMETRIC ASSESSMENT

This form of assessment provides information on the opinions and attitudes of pupils towards other pupils. It gives some guide to the pupil's level of acceptance by their peers.

Pupils can be asked who they would like to work and play with in a group. Alternatively they can be asked directly who they like or dislike. Finally, they can be asked to describe the personality and behaviour of particular pupils. The information derived from sociometry can be useful in interventions that aim to reintegrate pupils into peer groups.

THE ASSESSMENT PROCEDURE

Once you have selected your method of assessment then it is advisable to go through the following procedure:

- Identify the pupil's specific behaviour problems in consultation with staff, carers and the pupil.
- Choose practicable and appropriate assessment techniques which are agreeable to all involved.
- Find out the locations, frequency, duration and intensity of the pupil's behavioural problems.
- Identify the pupil's strengths and weaknesses in terms of resolving problems and the time scale involved - i.e. evaluating the pupil's level of cognitive and social skills and what the pupil needs to learn and how long that will take.
- Consider the pupil's level of self-confidence / perceived level of self-efficacy and attributional style.
- Determine whether the pupil possesses the motivation to change.
- Arrive at a formulation based on the assessment.

COGNITIVE FORMULATION

DEFINITION

Formulation is the process of arriving at an **hypothesis** as to the cause or reason for a pupil's behaviour problem and what factors are maintaining that problem.

The elements of cognitive assessment include the following techniques:

SELF-REPORT *OBSERVATION* *INTERVIEWS*

BEHAVIOUR RATING SCALES

as well as the following modes of analysis:

SELF-CONCEPT *TASK PERFORMANCE*

SOCIOMETRIC *ATTRIBUTIONAL STYLE*

The formulation should lead to specific interventions for the problem.

FORMULATION

A cognitive formulation should combine the following elements:

- A brief and specific **description** of the pupil's problem behaviour.
- Suggested **reasons** for the development of his problem behaviour i.e. those **internal** and **external** cognitive factors which have contributed to the development of his problem. These will include in turn **predisposing** and **precipitating** elements.
- **Maintaining factors**: those cognitive factors serving to prolong the problem.

AN EXAMPLE

The following example concerns a NC year 7 boy.

DESCRIPTION

The boy refuses to answer questions from a class textbook when asked by the History teacher.

REASONS – Internal

He has had reading difficulties from an early age. He has low self-esteem – thoughts and feelings of embarrassment and shame. He attributed his failure to read to lack of ability.

REASONS – External

There is parental criticism due to his lack of progress in reading at his primary school and an unfavourable comparison with his younger sister who reads well. They attributed his failure to read well to his lack of ability.

MAINTAINING FACTORS

His continuing reading problems leads him to want to avoid further failure and therefore to avoid work. This compounds the problem and generates a very low level of self-efficacy and poor self-esteem. This is intensified by the continued parental criticism and negative comparisons.

The teacher further confirms his feelings of failure by asking him to read a textbook that is too difficult.

His peers taunt him over his reading difficulties which leads him to want to avoid school altogether. He feels embarrassed in front of his peers as he compares himself unfavourably to them.

All this confirms even more his perceived low self-efficacy and poor self-esteem.

This formulation should lead to particular interventions:

- Intensive help for his reading difficulties which could include peer-tutoring in school and paired reading at home. These interventions could serve two aims i.e. to increase his reading skills and to involve his peers and parents so helping to change their negative perceptions and feelings towards him into more positive ones.
- Increasing his self-esteem and self-efficacy by acknowledging and developing his particular strengths e.g. in Art and Technology.
- Differentiation of the work – the teacher could provide the pupil with a differentiated worksheet or approach that enabled the pupil to experience some success with the task.

COGNITIVE THERAPIES

THE THERAPIES

Such interventions or therapies can take the form of a **hybrid** or an **integration** of cognitive and behavioural approaches.

RATIONAL-EMOTIVE THERAPY (RET)

Devised by **Albert Ellis** this approach (recently renamed Rational-Emotive-Behaviour Therapy) assumes that cognitive processes and emotion are interconnected. It is based on the premiss that behaviour problems arise through **maladaptive** thinking or **irrational** thought. Inadequate thinking leads pupils to behave inappropriately. If pupils can be encouraged to develop rational ways of thinking about themselves and their problems then this will lead to more appropriate behaviour. An example is where a pupil thinks that because a particular teacher dislikes them, then all teachers do – a process of **unwarranted generalization**.

Another pupil may think inaccurately that their behaviour is controlled by **external forces** over which they have no control or that they lack control over their own behaviour. They think solely in terms of an **external locus of control** when they need to be thinking in terms of an **internal locus of control** realizing they can achieve changes in behaviour through their own efforts.

According to Ellis's **ABC** model, **problem behaviours** or **consequences** (C) are influenced by a person's **cognitive processes** e.g. beliefs (B) regarding particular **activating events** (A).

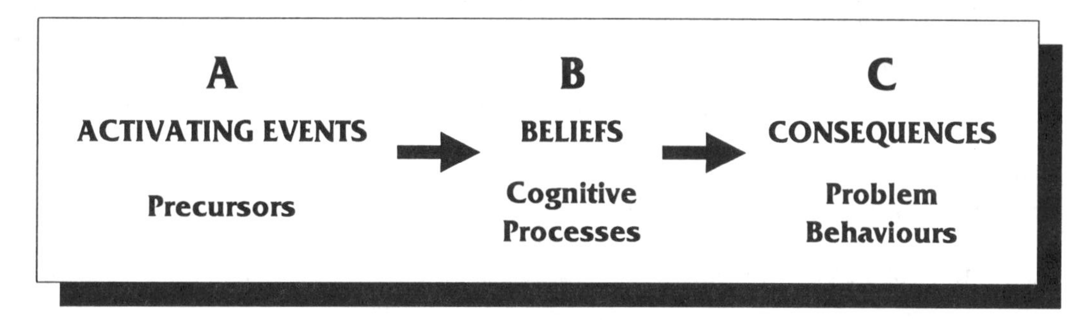

Thus the aim of this type of intervention is to identify and challenge the **distorted** or **irrational** thinking that leads to emotional and behavioural difficulties. Emotional and behavioural problems are seen as resulting from **absolutistic** and **dichotomous** thinking. This type of thinking takes the form of unconditional and dogmatic beliefs which are termed **cognitive distortions** or **irrational beliefs**.

Ellis identified **12 basic irrational beliefs** that result in unrealistic or unqualified expectations e.g. a tendency to think in terms of absolutes, that is in terms of 'musts' ('*I **must** do this perfectly*').

Some common cognitive distortions are:

- **Unwarranted generalization** from the particular to the general.
- **Guessing** rather than reasoning about what might happen.
- **Concentrating on the negative** aspects of oneself.
- **Minimizing one's achievement**.
- **Negative feelings** dominating one's thoughts
- **Perpetually seeking perfection** in oneself and one's performance

RET assumes that by substituting unrealistic and unqualified expectations with realistic ones changes in both feelings and behaviour can occur.

RET therapists use a variety of interventions: e.g. logical and empirical questioning of irrational thinking, self-monitoring of thinking, role playing, modelling, relaxation, operant conditioning and skills training.

COGNITIVE THERAPY (CT)

A. Beck sees emotional problems as being the result of **distorted** or **unrealistic** thinking about life. It is assumed that the way an individual processes information determines their feelings. It is necessary to consider the individual's view of their **self**, their **future** and their **world** - termed the **cognitive triad**.

Each individual possesses a **schema**, an organizing principle, which reflects that person's beliefs. When schemas are activated, negative **automatic thoughts** (a kind of internal monologue or running commentary on one's experience occurs) can arise along with distortions in the way information is processed.

These distortions affect perception, recall, inference and long-term memory and are called **cognitive deficits** or **errors**.

Common cognitive errors are:

- **Arbitrary inference** - jumping to conclusions.
- **Selective abstraction** - focusing on one thing to the exclusion of other pertinent factors.
- **Over-generalization** - generalizing from the particular to the general without good reason.
- **Magnification** and **minimization** - attributing too much or too little significance to events
- **Personalization** - relating events or incidents to oneself when there is no real connection.
- **Dichotomous thinking** - dividing up one's thinking or experience into either / or categories.

The individual examines their thinking for the presence of such errors and where identified take steps to rectify them. This requires self-monitoring.

CT therapists use a variety of techniques: monitoring of automatic thoughts and their validity, enabling clients to recognize the relationship between thoughts, feelings and behaviour, enabling clients to replace unrealistic with realistic thoughts and teaching clients how to identify and change their underlying belief system that leads to faulty thinking.

COGNITIVE INTERVENTIONS WITH PUPILS

A) SELF-INSTRUCTIONAL TRAINING

This particular cognitive intervention was developed by D. Meichenbaum who suggested that the development of control over one's behaviour involves a gradual move from external control to self-control through the internalization of instructions. Meichenbaum and Goodman (1971), developed a programme for dealing with impulsive behaviour in pupils. The aims were to train pupils in the use of **verbal self-instructions** and appropriate responses and to encourage them to **self-reinforce** those responses.

The steps in the intervention were as follows:

- modelling of the appropriate behaviour by the therapist with overt instructions
- pupil imitates the behaviour along with overt self-instruction
- pupil imitates and whispers self-instruction
- pupil imitates with covert self-instruction

Generally, interventions take the form of teaching the skills related to self-instruction:

- defining the problem behaviour
- looking at the approach to the problem
- looking at how to focus on the problem
- using coping statements for changing incorrect behaviours
- developing the process of self-reinforcement for appropriate behaviour

B) PROBLEM-SOLVING SKILLS TRAINING

D'Zurilla and Goldfied (1971) outlined a problem-solving approach that comprised five stages;

- orientation
- problem definition and formulation
- positing alternatives
- decision making
- verification

Problem-solving approaches involve training pupils in the specific skills of problem-solving. These skills are listed as follows:

- preventing initial impulsive responses – stopping and thinking
- identifying problems – ways of recognizing problems
- generating alternatives – brainstorming
- thinking about consequences
- planning a solution
- evaluating the plan

This type of problem-solving intervention has been used with pupils who are impulsive and disruptive.

This approach is also directed particularly at those pupils who experience problems in interpersonal relationships. The underlying assumption is that pupils with behaviour problems also lack the necessary cognitive skills which are seen as essential for appropriate interactions with teachers and other pupils. Pupils that engage in behaviours such as arguing and fighting are seen as not having learned alternative ways of behaving. For example, they may have acceptable goals but may choose undesirable strategies to achieve those goals.

The teacher can devise with the pupil, a **pupil behaviour plan**. This is a problem-solving plan that the pupil can follow (Bill Rogers' Behaviour Recovery is a good example). It can take the following form:

The teacher with the pupil:

- **Identifies** and **clarifies** the problem and the target behaviours e.g. they both agree that the pupil makes aggressive demands of other pupils and that the target behaviour should be one that takes the form of a non-aggressive approach to those pupils.

- **Considers alternative** ways of coping with the problem e.g. both agree that the pupil should offer to help or share something of their's with other pupils.

- **Outline the steps** required to achieve the desired behaviour e.g. arrange for the pupils concerned to be in a specific group.

- **Discuss the possible consequences** of behaving in certain ways e.g. offering help or sharing is more likely to gain positive attention whereas aggression is liable to antagonize other pupils and prevent the pupil from achieving their goal.

C) STRESS-INOCULATION TRAINING

Meichenbaum emphasized the importance of clients acquiring **coping skills** that enabled them to deal with small, manageable amounts of stress as a means to resolving larger problems. Once clients can tolerate small amounts of stress then it is assumed that they will be able to cope with increased amounts and also feel that they have greater self-control.

Meichenbaum and Cameron (1973), proposed a three-stage model:

- didactic instruction as to the nature of stress
- teaching coping skills, e.g. relaxation techniques, use of positive self-statements and self-reinforcement
- exposure to stressful events enables the client to practise their newly acquired coping skills (behaviour rehearsal)

This approach has been used with pupils as a means of controlling anger.

Pupils can also be provided with a **self-control monitoring sheet** to enable them to record their thoughts, feelings and behaviour about situations which lead them to engage in inappropriate behaviour e.g. a loss of self-control when angry. This form can help the pupil to reflect on their problem and thereby put them in a better position to control the behaviour.

D) ATTRIBUTION RETRAINING

This approach developed by A. Bandura and M. L. Weiner emphasizes how the pupil's causal explanations for their problems have certain consequences i.e. for the persistence of that behaviour and for expectations about the future. When pupils make incorrect attributions about the cause of their problems these attributions adversely affect their performance. Pupils may see the problem as being caused by other pupils or by teachers and that they have no responsibility for their behaviour. Where they accept responsibility they may claim they have no control over their behaviour.

Attribution retraining is directed at encouraging such pupils to accept that with effort they are able to effect control over their behaviour so facilitating those pupils' beliefs in their own **self-efficacy**. Pupils are encouraged to reflect on their behaviour and to develop strategies that draw on their own resources thus helping them to attribute changes to their efforts rather than seeing change as due to factors beyond their control.

SOCIAL LEARNING PERSPECTIVE

Social learning model

This perspective developed by **A. Bandura** and, **W. Mischel** sees behaviour, cognitive processes and the environmental factors as interconnected and as influencing each other (**Reciprocal Determinism**). Individuals can influence their environment as well as being influenced by their surroundings. The difference between the social learning approach and the behavioural approach is that the latter reinforces particular actions whereas the former contributes to the acquisition of new behaviours.

The pupil is seen as active in using cognitive processes to represent events and is deemed capable of free choice and self-control. Pupils may be influenced by their environment but they are also able to choose how to behave. They are in a position to formulate expectations as to the future but these expectations can also be influenced by reinforcement and sanctions.

A pupil's **behaviour** is seen as influenced by:

- The **goals** or **plans** they have – in terms of choosing particular priorities and actions.
- Their **self-concept** – which refers to particular cognitive processes e.g. self-control, self-reinforcement and self-criticism.
- Their **self-efficacy** perceptions – which is their perceived capability of coping with particular problems in specific situations. These perceptions influence the pupil's thinking, feelings, motivation and actions.
- **Observational** learning – this form of learning is where a pupil learns by observing others. The person observed is termed a **model**. This form of learning includes the following elements:

Attention depending on which model the pupil selects and how accurately they are perceived.

Retention depending on how much the pupil remembers for the purposes of practising or rehearsing the modelled behaviours.

Motor Reproduction depending on the pupil possessing the relevant learning skills in order to reproduce the model's behaviour.

Motivation depending on the pupil's desire to reproduce the model's behaviour.

This form of learning is seen as explaining the origin of new behaviour.

- **Vicarious learning:** this form of learning occurs where a pupil acquires particular thoughts and feelings after observing a model and identifying with the model's feelings.
- **Self-regulation:** a pupil's behaviour is determined by expectancies or what they anticipate might happen in the future. There are **outcome expectations** where a pupil estimates that particular behaviours will result in certain outcomes or consequences and **efficacy expectations** where a pupil believes they can successfully perform the desired behaviour.
- **Self-reinforcement:** a pupil reinforces their behaviour according to goals they have set for themselves.

Overall a pupil's behaviour is seen as not only influenced by the environment but by consequences that they create for themselves.

SOCIAL LEARNING INTERVENTIONS

MODELLING

- **Structure in stages**
- **Incorporate feedback**
- **Be clear and easily understood**
- **Rehearse the pupil until a satisfactory level is reached**

The teacher demonstrates the desired behaviour to the pupil and the pupil imitates that behaviour until they reach an appropriate level of performance. The teacher should also verbalise about the demonstration as it is given. In addition the teacher may need to reinforce the efforts of the pupil. The pupil should be encouraged to use **positive self-statements** in order to increase motivation.

The model should possess the following characteristics:

BE REALISTIC *CONVEY TRUST*

BE CONVINCING *HAVE SUFFICIENT STATUS*

CHANGING PERCEIVED SELF-EFFICACY

A pupil may experience low levels of self-efficacy. This means that they have low expectations of being successful in particular situations. The aim of an intervention would be to improve a pupil's perceived self-efficacy. This could be achieved by using modelling, self-instructional statements, self-reinforcement and attribution retraining.

COGNITIVE EVALUATION

Cognitive evaluation will focus on changes in cognitive processes that have occurred during the intervention: some form of cognitive restructuring. This means looking at the positive changes in a pupil's beliefs, attitudes, expectations, attributions and perceived self-efficacy. Positive changes in the cognitive process will hopefully be correlated with appropriate changes in behaviour. Behavioural evaluation will help to establish that changes in behaviour have also occurred.

A positive change in a pupil's cognitive processes would be where a pupil believes that they have within them the power to change their behaviour through their own efforts. Another positive change would be where a pupil no longer always blames others for getting into trouble.

A baseline should be established in terms of the pre-intervention beliefs, attitudes, expectations etc. of the pupil so that comparisons may be made at a later date when the intervention is at an end. It should be possible to see if there has been, for example, an increase in perceived self-efficacy or that reattribution has occurred.

Date ( ) Day ( )

Period ( ) Lesson ( )

Did you arrive on time?

Yes *Nearly* *No*

Did anybody bother you?	Did you keep your temper?
A bit / A lot	*Yes / No*
A bit / A lot	*Yes / No*
A bit / A lot	*Yes / No*
A bit / A lot	*Yes / No*
A bit / A lot	*Yes / No*

Could you do the work?

Not much *Some* *Most*

What did you do well?

( )

Example of a sheet from a Self-Monitoring Book

The Ecosystemic Perspective

THE ECOSYSTEMIC MODEL

This approach to behaviour problems focuses on the different ways in which people **perceive the world** and their **understanding of the interactions** in which they are involved. It also means looking at the different **systems** people are in and their mutual influence.

Emphasis is placed on the **context** in which the interactions and behaviours occur.

In order to understand interactions it is necessary to see how they relate to the context in which they occur.

SYSTEMS THEORY

The Ecosystemic perspective is based on **Systems Theory** (L. von Bertalanffy, 1950, 1968) which sees for example a school as being a system in itself and as interconnected to other systems. Changes in one system will have effects on another system e.g. changes in family systems can impact on schools as systems and school systems can react by impacting on family systems. Changes in a part of a system can affect another part of the same system e.g. a change in the pastoral organisation of the school can have an impact on classroom behaviour and classroom behaviour can in turn affect the pastoral system. This circular action and reaction of systems is an example of **recursive causality** where systems and sub-systems influence each other i.e. a **mutuality** of influence. Interactions between members of the systems can be seen **reciprocal** that is a teacher influences a pupil and the pupil influences the teacher.

FAMILY THERAPY

This approach also draws on a **family therapy** model which is an example of the application of Systems theory.

There are different **schools** of family therapy e.g. Minuchin's Structural School and the Milan School. The Structural approach focuses on problems with family boundaries e.g. disengagement and enmeshment; the Milan approach, on family avoidance strategies and the Strategic approach, on family interactions that maintain behaviours.

My Mum is Brilliant.
I go out with her to get shopping.

Family therapy sees people as relating to one another through a desire for recognition and for a sense of belonging. People relate to one another within particular systems and they also relate to other systems. People help through their actions to maintain systems. In doing so an individual may suffer as a consequence. For example parents may displace family conflict on to a particular child within the family. If the child is having behaviour problems in school the parents then see this as confirming their opinion of the child and respond negatively. The parents' reaction helps to preserve their relationship at the expense of one of their children. The school in turn feels justified in their treatment of the child given the parents' agreement.

Another example is where a teacher displaces their feelings of incompetence in classroom management on to a particular misbehaving child and locates in that child the reason for classroom disruption.

The approach of family therapy seeks to understand relationships within the family as a product of interactions between the members of that family. Through these interactions the behaviour of family members is rewarded or punished and as a consequence their behaviour is encouraged or suppressed.

In this situation the family therapy approach examines the nature of the interactions between families and how those members perceive those interactions.

The family therapy approach has also been applied to the school system in the sense of seeing the school as being a part of a **triangular** relationship between the family, the child and the school. For example parents may come to value the problem behaviour of their child in school as a way of displacing on to the school the negative feelings they have in their relationship. Another example would be where a child displaces the negative feelings they have for a parent on to a particular teacher who reprimands them for bad behaviour.

THE ECOSYSTEMIC APPROACH TO BEHAVIOUR

This approach considers behaviour problems in school to be the product of interactions between teachers and pupils and between pupils themselves. These interactions occur in a certain context e.g. a particular classroom, and should be understood as being a function of the specific context. But from this perspective it is necessary to consider the possible **influence of wider systems**.

At the first level of analysis behaviour problems will be seen as resulting from particular interactions that are happening in the here-and-now e.g. in the classroom situation. This analysis can be facilitated by the use of the ABC or Functional Analysis.

At the second level the analysis will be widened to include the influences of other systems on the classroom situation e.g. how family conflict impacts on classroom behaviour or how behaviour difficulties at school affect family relationships.

This approach also emphasises the **interconnectedness** of all events in terms of **cycles**

of cause and effect. Behaviour problems are seen as resulting from a series of actions and reactions which although appearing as problems for a teacher may be seen by the pupil as a means of resolving their own particular difficulties. The pupil may continue to repeat the inappropriate behaviour because it is a means of coping with their own problem e.g. a pupil may keep getting out of their seat to avoid negative feelings arising from being unable to cope with the set task. The teacher's attempt to confront the pupil perpetuates the conflict because the teacher's response fails to deal with the problem as perceived by the pupil which in the pupil's eyes is the set task.

This perspective sees an intervention as needing to take into consideration the perceptions and behaviour of all the parties involved with the problem behaviour. In the school context teachers should reflect on their own perceptions and behaviour and how these may be contributing to a pupil's behaviour problems. The aim of an ecosystemic approach is to defuse confrontation by facilitating positive interactions between teachers and pupils. This requires the participants to engage in a non-judgmental, problem-solving analysis that avoids self-perpetuating cycles of negative interactions.

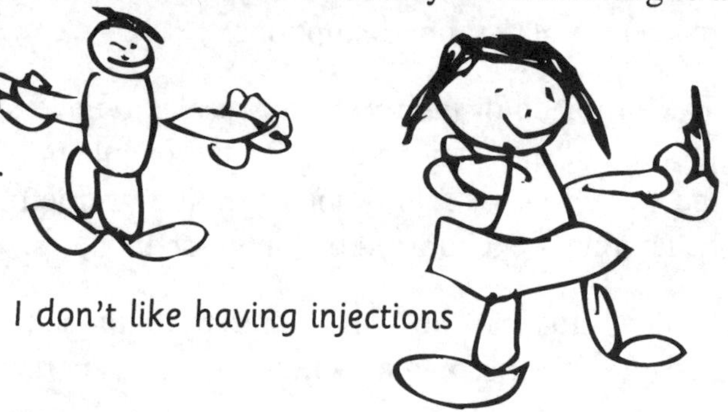

ECOSYSTEMIC ASSESSMENT

DEFINITION

This form of assessment looks at the pupil and their particular **environments** or **systems** (e.g. peer group, classroom, school organization and home.)

THE RATIONALE

The reason for this form of assessment is that a pupil can be positively or negatively influenced by any one or all of those environments or systems.

A pupil's behaviour may vary according to the environment or system being experienced. The reactions of significant others and interactions with them (e.g. peers, staff and carers) can affect the pupil's behaviour by increasing or decreasing its frequency and duration. A pupil may as it were become locked into a vicious circle of negative interactions leading to deteriorating behaviour.

Often the focus of an assessment is purely on the pupil to the exclusion of other factors. The exclusion of other factors may prevent the construction of a more valid assessment of the pupil's behaviour.

It may be necessary to look at the teacher's beliefs attitudes, expectations and inferences about the pupil in order to fully assess the pupil.

THE PROCESS

The process should include the collection of information about the pupil's interactions with their various environments or systems and how the pupil perceives those interactions.

Assessment in the first instance will be based on undertaking an analysis of the different kinds of interactions that occur within the school and between families and the school.

The classroom context: interactions between pupils and pupils and teachers e.g. pupils wind each other up by mutual name-calling and teachers and pupils escalate conflict by arguing over whether a pupil had verbally abused another pupil.

The family-school context: interactions between families and the school e.g. a pupil who is always being reprimanded by a particular teacher goes home depressed and a parent who blames the school when it excludes her child.

An analysis of the context will describe the interactions without attributing blame or searching for a definitive cause for the behaviour.

An analysis of behaviour difficulties will include understanding how the participants perceive the behaviour of all those involved. In other words, what meanings they attribute to the behaviour causing concern.

An example might be: a pupil who is continually out of seat and being rebuked by the teacher.

> **The teacher** may see this behaviour as simply disobedience or rudeness and therefore unjustifiable.
>
> **The pupil** may perceive it as a means of avoiding work that is too difficult and therefore justifiable.
>
> **Some pupils** may see the teacher as unfair in ignoring the pupil's learning difficulties.
>
> **Other pupils** may see the pupil as disrupting their learning.
>
> **The parents** may see the teacher as being annoyed with their child because of the demands the child's learning difficulties place on the teacher's time.
>
> **The teacher** may view the parents as colluding with the child to excuse what the teacher sees as the parents' poor upbringing of the child.

ASSESSMENT

Information should be collected on:

ENVIRONMENTS

- the pupil's specific environments (e.g. classroom, school and home).
- the locations where the problem behaviour occurs and where it is absent (e.g. particular lessons and places in school).

EXPECTATIONS

- expectations held by peers, staff and carers who perceive the pupil as a problem and those who do not.

INTERACTIONS

- positive and / or negative interactions between the pupil and significant others.

SKILLS

- the strengths and weaknesses the pupil possesses in terms of increasing positive behaviour.

ANALYSIS

- using the accumulated information to arrive at an assessment,which leads in turn to a **formulation** in terms of environmental influences on the pupil's behaviour,
- specific interventions that focus on environmental or systemic influences on the pupil's behaviour.

SPECIFIC TECHNIQUES

OBSERVATION

Observations in the relevant context should be undertaken with the aim of describing interactions in objective terms. This can be achieved using a Fixed Interval Sampling Sheet, a Behaviour Frequency Sheet and the ABC Sheet. These sheets enables the observer to describe the behaviour in terms of its duration and frequency and in terms of its antecedents and consequences, the ABC analysis (see '*Assessing Individual Needs*' in this series).

The perceptions of different observers can be compared with the observational data to see if any conclusions can be derived that will be useful in terms of an intervention. For example observation may show that the teacher's perceptions of a pupil's out of seat behaviour are incorrect in terms of the amount of time and number of times the pupil is out of their seat. Observation might also show that the pupil is genuinely having difficulty with the set task. Observational data when fed back to the teacher may lead to a positive change in the teacher's perceptions and behaviour towards the pupil. This in turn could lead the pupil to interact more appropriately with the teacher.

CHECKLISTS and RATING SCALES

These instruments can be used to obtain judgments made about the pupil by teachers and carers e.g. the Primary and Secondary Assessment Profiles can be used by teachers to record and collate information about the pupil's behaviour, (see *'Assessing Individual Needs'* in this series).

SOCIOMETRIC TECHNIQUES

This technique, largely devised by J. L. Moreno, is a means of discovering how far the pupil is accepted by the peer group and the structure and relationships within the group. Pupils can be asked to nominate other pupils as either friends, helpers or those they reject. This technique can help teachers identify the dominant pupils, the different sub-groups and those pupils who are rejected.

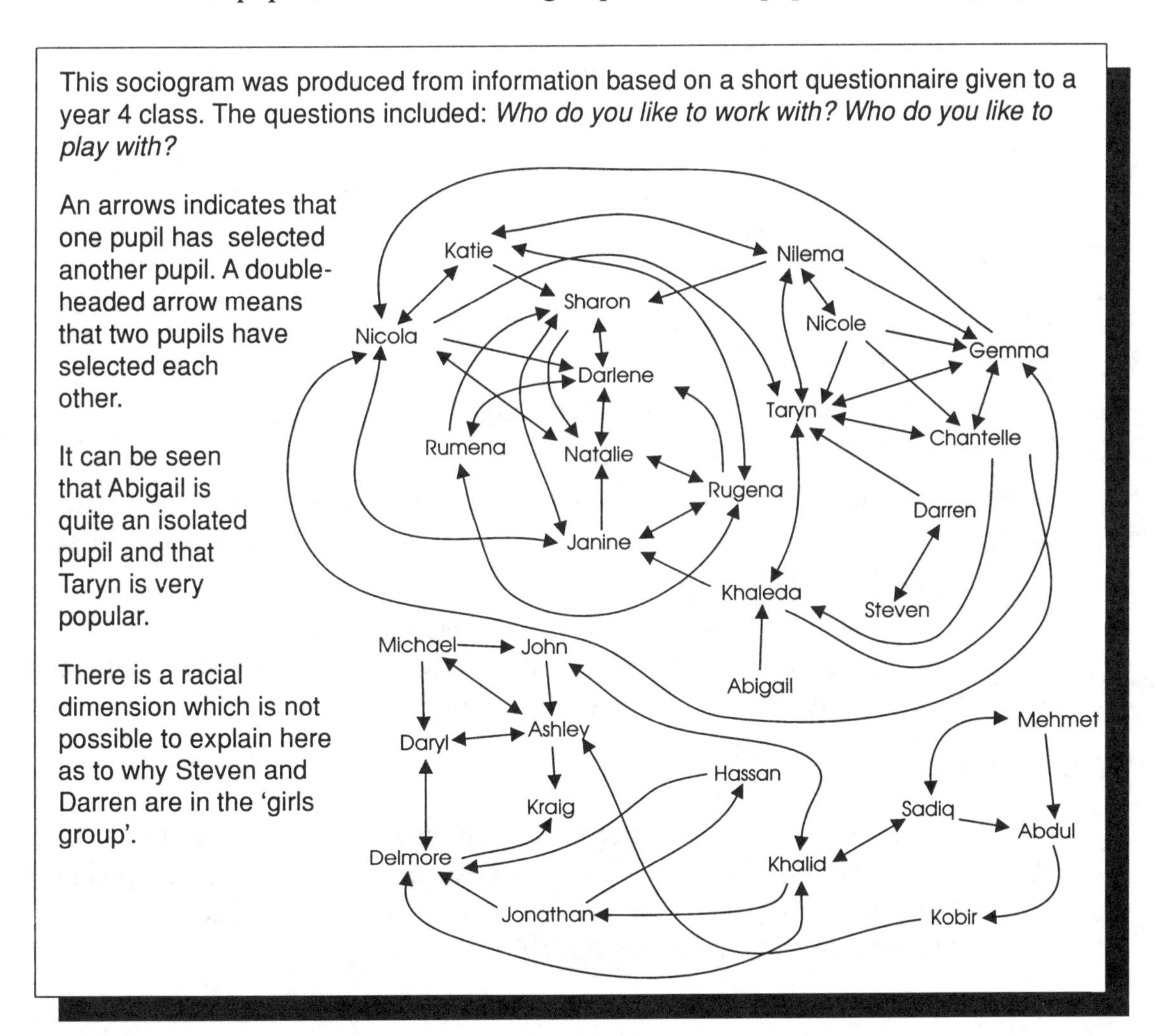

This sociogram was produced from information based on a short questionnaire given to a year 4 class. The questions included: *Who do you like to work with? Who do you like to play with?*

An arrows indicates that one pupil has selected another pupil. A double-headed arrow means that two pupils have selected each other.

It can be seen that Abigail is quite an isolated pupil and that Taryn is very popular.

There is a racial dimension which is not possible to explain here as to why Steven and Darren are in the 'girls group'.

Self-reports can also be used to find out how a pupil views their interactions with others.

Another method is the **Q-SORT procedure** (devised by W. Stephenson) where a pupil sorts out from presented statements what they would like to be (**the ideal self**) and what they think they are (**the actual self**). The teacher then compares the two for discrepancies and considers the implications of any discrepancies in terms of an intervention e.g. raising the pupil's self-esteem.

EXPLORING IN-SCHOOL FACTORS

This requires looking at the teaching environment in the classroom and how that might be affecting the pupil's behaviour e.g. **teaching style,** formality of **teaching methods**, **differentiation** of approach and materials, **seating** and **grouping** arrangements and behavioural **management** techniques.

It also involves looking at the type of teacher-pupil interactions in the classroom as well as pupil-pupil interactions.

FAMILY FACTORS

This requires looking at how families perceive the school and the school's perceptions of the family i.e. family – school interactions.

Families may perceive the pupil's problems as arising from the particular strategies the school uses with the pupil and also see the problem as the school's responsibility. The family may not experience any problem with the pupil at home or alternatively deny there is any problem.

The school may attribute the pupil's problem to the family background, situation or to family dynamics.

The family and school may resolve their differences and decide that the problem resides solely within the pupil.

However if the conflict in family and school perceptions persists then the situation needs to be assessed in terms of how it will be incorporated in a formulation and what its implications are for intervention.

The assessment should also consider what the consequences will be if perceptions of the participants remain unchanged. The consequences could be continued escalation, confrontation and the repetition of failed strategies.

FINAL POINTS

The assessment should also consider how the problem behaviour can be seen as positive by some or all of the participants. For example from the teacher's point of view the pupil's out of seat behaviour signals to the teacher the need to do something about the pupil's learning difficulties.

Finally the analysis of the problem has to be one that all the participants can agree on otherwise an intervention will flounder due to the continuation of conflicting perceptions and behaviour. For example if the teacher and the pupil can agree that the pupil's out of seat behaviour is related to the difficulty of the work then an intervention based on this agreement can be successfully implemented.

ECOSYSTEMIC FORMULATION

This type of formulation would result from an assessment which includes the various environments or systems that are perceived as influencing the pupil's behaviour, this will include pupil-pupil, teacher-pupil and teacher-parent interactions.

A pupil's problem behaviour may result from a combination of:

- **Within-pupil factors** e.g. reading difficulties.
- **Peer-group perceptions** e.g. other pupils perceiving the pupil as 'thick', as a consequence the pupil perceiving this as unpopularity becomes aggressive towards the peer group, this escalating into a cycle of negative interactions.
- **Teacher perceptions** e.g. the teacher perceiving the pupil as incapable of change and always expecting the pupil to present negative behaviour.
- **Teaching environment** e.g. the teacher sits the pupil on their own, the pupil feeling even more isolated and stigmatized.
- **Family perceptions** e.g. the family perceives the pupil as being victimized by the school and as a result challenges the school's negative perceptions of the pupil and encourages the pupil to resist negative labelling.

The pupil's problems are seen as due to a number of external factors besides the within-child factor of reading difficulties. The problems result from interactions between environments or systems.

In this example the pupil's problems can be seen as resulting from interactions between internal and external factors i.e. within-pupil factors and teacher, peer and family perceptions as well as the teaching environment.

Interventions need to be directed at or focused on the different systems involved in influencing the pupil's behaviour.

ANALYSIS OF INTERACTIONS SHEET

Name: *John Doe* **Age:** *11* **Date:** *1 1 94*

Form / Class: *Form 7R* **NC Year:** *7*

1) Describe how you perceive the interactions between yourself and the target pupil
in positive as well as negative terms

In negative terms: I see John as abusive and rude towards me particularly when I ask him to do some work, pay attention or to stop shouting out to other pupils.
in positive terms: I find that John on the rare occasion will ask me to help him with his work and even thank me afterwards.

2) Describe how other staff perceive the target pupil
in positive as well as negative terms

In negative terms: Some teachers say he is just the same in their lessons, rude and abusive. These teachers take him for Maths and Science. I gather from them that he has difficulty with the work. In positive terms: Some teachers say he is not a behaviour problem in their lessons and gets on with his work and is not rude to them. These teachers take him for practical subjects such as Art whereas I take him for French which he finds difficult.

3) Describe how you perceive the interactions between the target pupil and other pupils
in positive as well as negative terms

In negative terms: Some pupils dislike him because he interferes or distracts them from their work when he talks to them. He appears somewhat isolated. But others find him a laugh and would follow his lead if I didn't intervene.
In positive terms: One pupil sometimes helps him with his work and when this happens he tends to behave pleasantly to some of the other pupils as well.

4) Describe how you perceive the interactions within the target pupil's family and between the family and the school

John comes from family which is hostile to the school and towards me in particular. He has brothers who have attended this school and who have had me as their French teacher. They have also been rude and abusive. The parents always appear to take the side of their children when they come up to school but also complain about their children's rudeness towards them at at home.

The Ecosystemic Approach Analysis of Interactions Sheet

5) Describe any comparisons you are able to make between any observations undertaken of the target pupil: does this comparison highlight discrepencies or agreements. If so, what implications does it have for your picture of the pupil?

John does get on better in practical subjects where he is not asked to do so much reading and writing and where he can use his hands. However in other subjects like Science or Maths he is just the same as he is in French. I use to think that John was rude and abusive towards all the teachers but I found that he tends to be like that in lessons where he has learning difficulties even though the teachers have different personalities than mine. My picture then is of a pupil whose behaviour changes according to the subject he takes. His behaviour does not seem to relate to the personality of the teacher.

6) From the above information, summarise your perceptions and those of others and state your expectations of the target pupil.

I see John as behaving acceptably in some lessons because he can cope with the work and finds the subject interesting but in other subjects like mine he finds the work too difficult and resents being asked to get on with his work. If I left him alone I probably wouldn't be abused but then he would distract others and I would have to intervene.

7) If possible, REFRAME those perceptions in such a way that the target pupil's problem is redefined more positively. Describe your 'reframing'.

John is a pupil who experiences behavioural difficulties in the context of those lessons where his literacy and numeracy skills are found wanting. His behaviour can be positive in other lessons whatever the personality of the teacher. John can show a better side to his nature and I now recognize that, I probably need to make French more accessible and enjoyable for him by enabling him to use his practical skills, by sitting him with a peer tutor and by giving him more individual support. His misbehaviour may be his way of trying to bring this to my attention.

The Ecosystemic Approach Analysis of Interactions Sheet

ECOSYSTEMIC INTERVENTIONS

These types of interventions are ones proposed by **Molnar and Lindquist** (1989) and are based on the idea that all the participants through their interactions with each other in some way contribute to the problem behaviour. This approach asks all the parties involved to reflect on their behaviour in relation to the problem. Teachers should examine their perceptions of the pupil and the problem as should the pupil. The aim of this kind of intervention is to avoid confrontations between teachers and pupils by eliciting co-operation.

The teacher is asked to provide a behavioural analysis of the problem which entails being specific about the problem i.e. giving a precise description of the behaviour along with its context, frequency, duration and any antecedents and consequences.

The basis of this type of intervention is the use of alternative interpretations to explain problem behaviour. The overall aim is to provide a positive interpretation that terminates the negative cycle of successive escalation and confrontation. A positive interpretation is one that redefines the problem behaviour as one not of conflict but as one that is possibly serving a useful function within the particular interaction.

Sleuthing

The teacher is also asked to describe their perceptions of the pupil, the pupil's behaviour and interactions with others and the expectations they have of the pupil's behaviour. If possible the teacher should try to perceive the pupil's behaviour positively. The aim of positive interpretations is ultimately to facilitate a new cycle of interactions between teachers and pupils which both parties can perceive as a fresh beginning.

Reframing

This particular intervention is based on the idea that there are different, possible interpretations of the same behaviour or situations and that the behaviour of teachers and pupils will reflect those differing interpretations. If interpretations change then behaviour will change and if behaviour changes then interpretations will change.

For example if the pupil is out of seat the teacher may interpret it as simply defiance or alternatively as being due to the pupil having difficulty with the work and fearing failure. Based on the first interpretation the teacher will continue to reprimand the pupil who even if quiet will still not be able to cope with the set task. However the teacher can place a positive interpretation on the behaviour in the sense of perceiving the out of seat behaviour as an appeal for help on the part of the pupil. If interpreted in this way then the situation can be turned from one of conflict to one of co-operation. The pupil will remain seated as the teacher now recognises the pupil's learning difficulties and responds accordingly by differentiating the task for the pupil and by giving the pupil attention. Confrontation will cease as both teacher and pupil agree that it is the pupil's learning difficulty that relates to the problem behaviour and that this difficulty needs resolving.

Positive Connotation of Function

This particular intervention is based on the idea that a problem behaviour can be interpreted as serving a positive function for the teacher. For example the pupil's out of seat behaviour can be read as an indication that the teacher needs to attend to cues in the classroom that require specific strategies related to learning difficulties.

Positive Connotation of Motive

This intervention is based on the idea that by leaving their seat the pupil is conveying a message to the teacher that it would be more productive if the teacher spends time with pupils who are on task. The teacher then sees the pupil as having a more positive character than before and this changes the teacher's attitude towards the pupil.

'Symptom Prescription' technique

The aim of this technique is for the teacher to ask the pupil to perform the problem behaviour in different circumstances whereby the problem behaviour achieves the goal the pupil desires.

Conclusion

In adopting this approach teachers have to be prepared to accept the basic presuppositions which are:

- that the problem is the product of interactions within or between systems and therefore the problem is not seen as simply one of some deficit in the pupil.
- the problem pupil is as it were 'constructed' by teachers i.e. teachers perceive particular pupils in certain ways and as a result label those particular pupils rather than others as 'disruptive'.
- that schools need to accept that they contribute to the problem by the kinds of interactions they promote with their pupils.

ECOSYSTEMIC EVALUATION

This type of evaluation requires a comparison between baselines and the end points of interventions. This is due to there being several levels of intervention.

With the ecosystemic approach the evaluation will need to encompass the various systems or environments and the interactions between them.

For example:

Positive and negative interactions between pupil and pupils, pupil and teachers and carers and teachers may need to be evaluated.

The changed perceptions of pupil, teachers and carers may also require evaluation.

Behavioural and cognitive assessment techniques and forms can be used to evaluate changes in interactions and perceptions of those involved in the interventions.

Observable changes in interactions can be recorded through the use of observation schedules.

Changes in perceptions can be elicited through questionnaires, rating scales and checklists.

The aim will be to see if e.g. reframing has occurred, that similar perceptions or attributions have emerged and that triangulation has been overcome.

Given that behaviour problems are seen as arising through negative interactions then evaluation should aim to establish that all the changes in the contributory systems have been evaluated.

The Psychodynamic Perspective

PREFACE

The **psychodynamic perspective** of behaviour locates the origin of the maladaptive behaviour in the **unconscious functioning of the psyche**. We have used the word 'psyche' rather than 'mind' (which can be and often is used interchangeably) as the latter tends to refer in psychology to the cognitive or conscious mental processes. For the most part, we are referring to emotional aspects and perceptions of the individual which may be unconscious in origin.

Due to considerations of volume, this chapter is restricted to outlining a limited number of concepts derived from the **psychoanalytical approach**. Our intention is to give the reader an introduction to the complex area of psychoanalytical theory as it relates to emotional and behavioural difficulties in the learning situation. Those readers interested in further study will find the bibliography useful.

When we refer to the **learning situation**, we mean the relationship of the pupil to both the **environment** in which the learning takes place (the institution, the teachers, peers) and the **learning task** itself (the curriculum content and presentation, individual on/off task behaviour).

We have chosen to concentrate on certain aspects of psychoanalytical theory which have a more immediate relevance to the learning situation in what they have to offer us as practising teachers. We have grouped these under the heading of:

Aspects of Psychoanalytical Approaches and their Implications for the Learning Situation

1. **Ego Defences in the Learning Situation (S. Freud)**
2. **Unconscious Phantasy and the Learning Situation (Melanie Klein)**
3. **Effects of Emotional Deprivation and Loss in the Learning Situation (J. Bowlby)**
4. **Transference and Counter-transference in the Learning Situation (S. Freud)**

This chapter does **not provide a guide to intervention** in the same way which the other chapters in this volume do. The previous chapters are useful in assisting the classroom practitioner and the institution in developing and evaluating interventions without considerable input from the specialist. Here, in contrast, we hope to offer a succinct guide to which aspects of psychoanalytical theory have relevance to day-to-day practice in the classroom and the larger institution of the school and which may assist those responsible for the management of schools, and teachers to reflect on preventative approaches. **Intervention in the fullest sense may ultimately remain the domain of the trained specialist**.

Nevertheless, it is hoped that the reader will gain a perspective from which to reflect on what may be occurring in the learning situation. This may enable the practitioner, through increased understanding, to better manage the stress which working with these pupils can create.

PERSPECTIVE SCHEMA	PSYCHODYNAMIC	APPLICATION TO LEARNING SITUATION
THEORETICAL BASIS	Unconscious processes seeking resolution of psychic conflict eg ego defences. Unconscious phantasy influences behaviour.	Aspects of the learning situation trigger unconscious processes; pupil still enmeshed in emotional conflict generated by earlier experiences.
MODEL OF THE PERSON	Behaviour is determined by unconscious processes	Behaviour has a meaning of which the pupil is not consciously aware but which directs/influences perceptions of self, others and the learning task
ASSESSMENT BASIS	Ego defences; unconscious phantasy; internal working model(s)	Defences; aspects of the interpersonal relationship between pupil and teacher, pupil and peers, pupil and school; characteristics of engagement with the learning task
ASSESSMENT PROCEDURE	Projective techniques; transference- relationship; defences / unconscious phantasies inferred.	Observation schedules; learning profiles; quality of engagement in the learning task; interviews; projective techniques; pupil's use of metaphor; transference-relationship with teacher and peers
FORMULATION BASIS	Unresolved unconscious conflicts / phantasies / inappropriate internal working models manifest in emotional and behavioural difficulties.	Learning difficulties arise from unresolved emotional difficulties caused by unconscious conflicts or pre-occupations
FORMULATION	Problem behaviour caused by unresolved unconscious conflicts / phantasies / internal working model arousing unconscious anxiety and ego defences	Aspects of the learning situation trigger anxiety. Maladaptive response has an unconscious component.
INTERVENTION BASIS	Facilitating insight; strengthening the ego.	Identifying and modifying where appropriate aspects of the learning situation which arouse pupil's anxiety. Increasing pupil's confidence in ability to manage aspects of the learning situation. Increase self-esteem
INTERVENTION STRATEGIES	Interpretation of resistances and defences or unconscious phantasy in and through the transference-relationship .	Working at one remove through use of metaphor; voicing pupil's feelings; play therapy, art, music and educational therapy; reducing threatening aspects of the learning situations; promoting self-esteem.
EVALUATION BASIS	Insight into unconscious conflict; ego-strength	Modification of maladaptive aspects of pupil's engagement in the learning situation as a result of emotional pre-occupations.
EVALUATION	Increased insight and ego-strength	Improved management of response to anxiety in the learning situation; more appropriate interaction with teacher and peers. More attention available to engage in learning task.

APPLICATION OF THE PSYCHODYNAMIC PERSPECTIVE TO THE LEARNING SITUATION

INTRODUCTION TO THE THEORY OF THE PSYCHODYNAMIC PERSPECTIVE

When engaged in the teaching of pupils whose behavioural difficulties originate in large part from maladaptive responses to the resolution of unconscious conflict (**psychodynamic perspective**), as opposed to maladaptive learning (**behavioural perspective**), maladaptive thinking (**cognitive/behavioural perspective**) or negative interactions (**ecosystemic perspective**), the class teacher may feel, quite appropriately, that the training they have received as teachers does not fully equip them to deal with the challenges which this particular type of pupil behaviour can present. Indeed, as previously stated, these pupils often need specialised interventions in order to facilitate meaningful behavioural change in the learning situation.

In **psychoanalytical theory** the origin of the emotional and behavioural difficulty is located in the earliest history of the child's development. The experiences encountered and unconscious phenomenon (e.g. ego defences, unconscious phantasy - see below) which the child has developed during this period, and which informs his perceptions of outer reality, is filtered through their inner world of emotions. These have remained, in part, unchanged or have failed to adapt to change real change in the outer world. The outer reality continues to be interpreted and processed as though it were in fact still part of the infantile/child's world. Events in the objective world of the older child trigger reactions which seem in many cases to belong to the behavioural repertoire of the infant or young child. From this perspective, the manifest behaviour is not perceived as a direct response to what is occurring objectively, but as related unconsciously to much earlier experience.

The psychodynamic approach is concerned with applying principles derived from psychoanalytical theory in an attempt to understand the meaning which the pupil invests in their understanding of the world. It is this which underlies aspects of their maladaptive behaviour. This meaning is not always accessible through the assessment techniques which apply in the other perspectives outlined elsewhere in this volume.

Psychoanalytical theory is extremely complex and there are many differences of opinion and debate around the functions and roles of the processes of the psyche. In what follows, we have aimed at giving the non-specialist an overview of those parts of the theory which have perhaps more relevance when it comes to the learning situation.

REFERRAL CHARACTERISTICS FROM THE PSYCHODYNAMIC PERSPECTIVE

This chapter is concerned with the pupil whose behaviour may present as :

- '**incomprehensible**' or '**inconsequential**' or '**puzzling**'
- **under-achieving** despite proven cognitive ability
- **immature** in comparison to others of the same age
- **phobic**
- **anxious, withdrawn** or **depressed**
- **hostile**
- **unpredictable** in terms of actions and reactions and where no obvious pattern emerges easily

Pupils with emotional and behavioural difficulties may also have specific learning difficulties. Unless these are assessed and specialist support given the pupil will not make progress. However as we have said above, sometimes the failure to achieve cannot be traced to a specific learning or cognitive difficulty. It is as if the pupil is not free to use his ability because he is consciously or unconsciously preoccupied by the 'muddle' caused by the emotional problem. While the pupil remains preoccupied by unresolved inner conflict he is unable to engage in the learning situation to the best of his ability. For this reason, the emotional difficulty is as much a special educational need as that associated with a specific learning difficulty and requires that we make provision for addressing it as such.

The teachers of pupils who might be described using some of the above definitions are often left feeling:

- **de-skilled, inadequate** or **helpless** to bring about change or impart skills
- **angry**
- **despairing**
- **anxious**
- **depressed**
- **isolated** or '**persecuted**' (as when a pupil seems to experience these difficulties with one teacher or group of teachers only and where others report no concerns)

As we will discuss later in the chapter, the way the teacher feels, or is made to feel, by this type of pupil behaviour is a significant part of the diagnostic picture. Of course, any teacher, on a 'bad' day, may feel all of the above with pupils who do not have extreme symptoms. It is the degree to which the teacher experiences these feelings, the duration of difficulty and its seeming resistance to modification or permanent change in the learning relationship which characterises the teaching of this pupil group.

ASPECTS OF PSYCHOANALYTICAL APPROACHES AND THEIR IMPLICATIONS IN THE LEARNING SITUATION

1. Ego defences in the learning situation (Freud)

i) Definition of The Ego

- The ego could be defined as that part of the individual's psyche which has the function of **differentiating**, **rationalising** or **controlling** the more primitive, unstructured or 'passionate' elements of the psyche which are experienced unconsciously as potentially overwhelming to the ego.

- The ego might be seen to act as a kind of psychological gatekeeper, **mediating** as it does between conflicting demands of the psyche and external reality which might be experienced unconsciously as a threat to its integrity.

- The ego will also act to preserve the individual's **sense of identity** which itself is seen to have worth. It may do this when certain **unacceptable aspects of the self** threaten to manifest themselves. Threats to the ego's sense of worth, or to its function as a kind of psychic 'cement' to the identity of the self, are experienced as threats to the existence of the individual and arouse anxiety.

ii) Ego Defences

- The ego uses defence mechanisms to protect its integrity and ability to continue to act as a mediator in the psyche .

- This defensive process is not seen to be maladaptive in itself. It is deemed maladaptive when the defensive response gives rise to behaviour which causes difficulties in the person's harmonious adaptation to reality.

- These defence mechanisms operate at an unconscious level as a response to anxiety and the individual is not, by definition, aware of them.

- The degree of ego-anxiety experienced as a result of conflict will differ from one individual to another, as will mechanisms for coping with this.

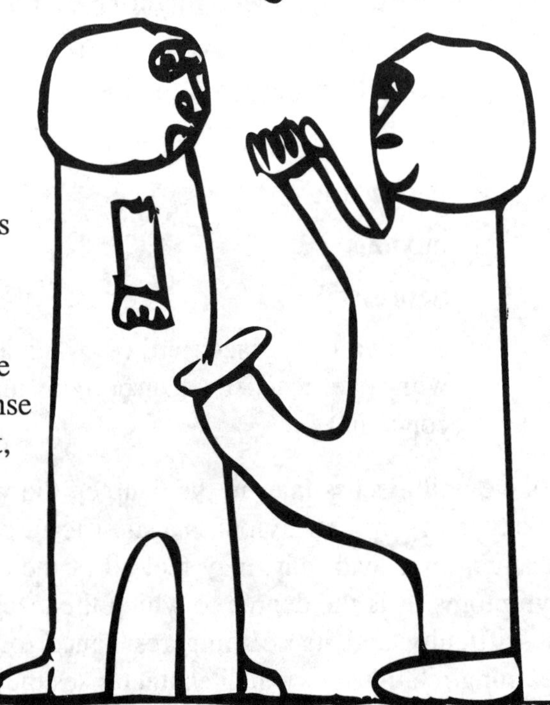

- When these strategies or mechanisms are used successfully, they do reduce tension. Their success reinforces their use and the person will begin to adopt positions which will have the effect of reducing ego-anxiety habitually. In other words the defences become part of what we loosely call the 'personality'.

> ***Freud's Analogy of the function of the Ego***
>
> *Sigmund Freud used the following analogy when referring to the function of the ego. He likened the primitive forces in the individual which are present from birth (passions, appetites, impulses which he termed the '**id**') to a horse and the **ego** is the rider on the back of this horse which attempts to master it. Both the psychic integrity of the person and his ability to respond appropriately to the demands of external reality, depends on how well the ego is able to master these primitive, irrational forces. Freud however goes on to say that whereas the rider uses his own strength to master the horse, the ego uses 'borrowed strength'. He is referring partly to the unconscious processes which the ego uses to defend itself against the threat of being overwhelmed by the primitive impulses.*

iii) Aspects of the learning situation which arouse ego defences

Certain aspects of the learning situation can provoke anxiety. Each act of learning requires a certain amount of risk-taking. Learning tasks can carry with them the potential for the accompanying or related risk of exposing the ego to anxiety e.g. in the form of a confrontation with the individual's limitations either short or long-term. The relationships with the teacher and peers can also provoke anxiety. Certain unconscious defences, or the degree to which they are used to defend against this anxiety, can hinder progress in the learning situation. The examples below indicate some aspects of the learning situation which may result in maladaptive responses arising from the unconscious defence used to cope with the anxiety.

Examples in the learning task:

- a task in which the pupil feels unconfident and where his sense of self-worth might be challenged through being seen to make mistakes

- persevering with a difficult task which involves the management of frustration and lack of immediate gratification
- feeling impotent or belittled in the face of not knowing
- tasks or topics which might bring the pupil into unconscious contact with aspects of his inner and outer life which create anxiety

Examples in the learning relationship with the teacher:

- having a new or temporary teacher where the boundaries and expectations are still unclear
- experiencing aspects of the teacher's role as reminiscent of aspects of other significant person's roles in the pupil's life (see transference and attachment below)
- being unsure about whether the teacher values the pupil as a person (see internal working models below)
- experiencing the teacher as comparatively more powerful or knowing and envying what knowledge, ability and skill they possess (see unconscious phantasies below)

Examples in the relationship with peers:

- not being able to master a new concept as quickly or as well as one's peers
- being able to master a task far better than one's peers and therefore giving rise to their envy or a self-image which conflicts with the values of the group
- experiencing feelings of rivalry for the attention of the teacher or other significant person

iv) **An example of an ego-defence which hinders learning**

Consider the instance of a pupil who is habitually slow to begin a task even though once launched he will complete the task successfully. We might think of him as 'lazy'. The **degree** of the teacher's exasperation due to the **duration** of a problem which has no rational explanation may indicate that there is an **unconscious element** at work here. We could think about this behaviour as a habitual **ego-defence**. The situation of beginning a task may, for example, raise **anxiety** about the ego's ability to cope with the **frustration** involved in getting it right. The child may adopt the 'lazy' approach as a means of gaining the reassurance and encouragement from the teacher at the start of the task. ('*Come on. You know you can do this*!' we say several times a week to this pupil often becoming exasperated in the end.) The child is momentarily using the **ego-defence of regression** whereby he returns to an earlier stage of **ego development** which is characterised, among other things, by a greater dependency on the teacher/carer. This reduces the relatively mild anxiety

EXAMPLES OF COMMON EGO-DEFENCES USED IN THE LEARNING SITUATION

The following list is not exhaustive. It can be seen that one defence tends to lead to another.

DEFENCE	DEFINITION	EXAMPLE IN THE LEARNING SITUATION
REGRESSION	Process whereby the individual avoids or seeks to avoid anxiety by partial or total return to an earlier stage of development	A pupil will revert to an immature mode of behaviour e.g. crying or rolling around on the floor in order to avoid tackling a task which he/she feels they will not be able to accomplish
DENIAL	Denying or forgetting painful feelings and events	A pupil who might be experiencing difficulty with a task will defend himself from feelings of belittlement by denying the difficulty and avoiding the task. For example: "This is too easy for me. This is baby stuff."
SPLITTING	When the person is denying unacceptable parts of himself, he may go on to use the defence of splitting this unacceptable part off and projecting it onto someone else. Splitting may also be used to describe the process whereby two or more significant others are endowed with opposing characteristics.	A pupil might accuse the teacher or a classmate of being e.g. hostile towards him when he is in fact feeling anxious about his own unconscious hostility towards them. The pupil's hostility is said to be split off. A pupil might behave towards one teacher(s) as if they are wonderful and towards another (others) as if they are awful.
PROJECTION	When a person experiences impulses or wishes or aspects of himself which are unacceptable, he might situate these in another (see denial)	A victim of bullying might be projecting his own aggressive impulses on to the bully
IDEALISATION	Idealisation might result in part from a mixture of denial, splitting and projection. The need for a perfect other results in the denial of less wonderful parts of the person. Idealisation is a defence against recognising faults in the other towards which one might experience envious or hostile or some other unacceptable feeling. By idealising the other one is freed from the guilt of these negative feelings but the result is a loss of self-esteem through comparison with the other.	A pupil may not reach his full potential in the learning situation where he feels unconscious envy of another pupil's success. This is defended against by idealising that pupil and belittling oneself in comparison. The other is better or even perfect and cannot be competed with.
RATIONALISATION	A process of giving an explanation for an action after the event in order to conceal its true motivation to oneself and others	A pupil who explains a failure to bring in homework because they had forgotten to take the right material home in the first place and thereby rationalise his own lack of responsibility or anxiety about being able to fulfil the task.
REACTION-FORMATION	This is a defence where an unacceptable impulse is controlled by exaggerating its opposite	A pupil who is extremely tidy might be concealing an inner feeling of messiness and "unpresentablity"

experienced enough for the pupil to engage in the task. Understanding this behaviour as an **unconscious coping strategy** and not a 'moral defect' in the child's personality or a deliberate **attention-seeking** provocation, allows it to be approached differently. It would be more accurate to describe the behaviour as '**attention-needing**' (a term becoming more current). This is not to say that the teacher should collude with what, however mild it may be, is a maladaptive response. The child may not be fully aware that this is what he does. The teacher may be able to highlight the behaviour with the child and explore alternative strategies with him.

It is easy to move from this example of the use of a defence mechanism which causes mild disruption to one where the anxiety is so great that simple encouragement will have no effect. The anxiety in some children before a new task or a return to one which has caused past anxiety can be extreme and give rise to a more intense and resistant ego-defence mechanism.

John is a 10 year old in NC Year 6. He has an average IQ. and has no specific learning difficulty. However he is at the beginning stages of reading and writing and uses diversionary tactics of disruption to avoid the anxiety he experiences when he is confronted with a task which he feels unable to manage. In fact, John has recourse to a number of ego-defences but here we shall concentrate on his use of regression.

At the start of the NC Year 6, after the summer holidays, John refused to return to school and ended up being literally dragged in, kicking and screaming, by his mother. When she felt able to leave, he collapsed in the corridor outside his classroom and began to wail loudly 'I want my mummy'. He was behaving very much as some children do when they are taken to nursery school and left there for the first time. It took weeks to settle John back into class, during which time he was able to avoid 'work' almost entirely, having a special programme set up for him where he was able to work at the level of a Reception child for the most part. In some ways then John achieved relief from the anxiety of failure by regressing to this earlier stage of ego development. However, this was achieved at the price of simultaneously re-activating the much earlier anxieties of this stage connected to separation from his mother (see the section on attachment). In connection with this it is perhaps relevant that from the age of three, John's parents' relationship began to breakdown ending in divorce with father leaving the family home when John was in Reception. As he never progressed much beyond this stage in terms of academic achievement, it would appear that his emotional and intellectual development became 'stuck' at this point.

2. Unconscious phantasy and the learning situation (Klein)

i) Definition of unconscious phantasy

- According to psychoanalytical thinking, infants, from the beginning of life, develop unconscious phantasies about all that they experience. (This does not refer to 'fantasies' of the day-dreaming type or conscious imaginings - hence the use of the different spelling.)
- Since the infant experiences most vividly through their bodily sensations and functions, these phantasies are, in the first instance, constructed from the biological processes of, for example, feeding, digestion and defecation. The infant develops certain phantasies around the experience of the mother, or rather her body. He does not, to begin with, experience her as a whole person but rather as parts of a body: the breast (or bottle which represents the breast) the face, etc.
- Certain unconscious phantasies may arouse anxiety which the ego seeks to master by developing defences (see above).
- As the infant grows and his mental processes develop, these unconscious phantasies do not cease to be active. As the infant develops, he constructs other unconscious phantasies around, for example the relationship between the mother and father (or substitute figures). Freud has explored the unconscious phantasies which contribute to what he called the Oedipus complex; unconscious phantasies around wishing to possess the parent of the opposite sex and eliminate the parent of the same sex.
- Psychoanalytical theory maintains that these unconscious phantasies continue throughout life to accompany conscious thought and indeed affect it.

ii) An example of unconscious phantasy

As we have stated above, unconscious phantasy is attached to all aspects of the infant's experience. Here, we look at some aspects of the phantasies around the infant's experience of feeding in particular:

- In the unconscious phantasy of the infant, the breast (or bottle) is experienced as the source of all that is good and nourishing, and, when this experience of feeding is good, it is associated in phantasy with life-giving properties.
- The breast is further experienced in unconscious phantasy as possessing something desirable and the mother who 'owns' the breast is felt to enjoy all the goodness which the breast bestows.

- Through the operation of this phantasy, the infant may come to envy the breast which the mother seems to be able to have 'all to herself'. The infant in relation to this may unconsciously experience a sense of lack of control and hostility towards the breast / mother and consequent anxiety and development of ego defences.

Using other perspectives is OK

The origin of the behaviour may be the attempt to cope with an unconscious conflict and this can give the teacher a perspective on the meaning of the behaviour. However, the intervention need not be drawn from the repertoire of psychodynamic technique. There is nothing to prevent the teacher drawing up a simple ***behaviour modification programme*** *from the behavioural repertoire or a self-regulation programme from the* ***cognitive approach****. Both of these interventions can help by motivating the child initially and by giving the child the experience of an alternative. It is only when the anxiety experienced is more severe the behavioural or cognitive approach, on their own, will 'draw a blank' so to speak and more specialist intervention may be indicated.*

In the case of John, a behaviour modification programme or a self-regulation programme could help to contain his behaviour to a certain degree in the short-term. However, the need to strengthen John's ego to enable him to progress from maladaptive defence mechanisms, i.e. to cater for John's emotional needs, would require a longer-term and more specialised intervention which ideally would also involve work with John's family.

iii) Examples of unconscious phantasy around feeding in the learning situation

We have chosen to concentrate here on the unconscious phantasies associated with the feeding experience. There are many others but space compels us to select.

- When the child is in the learning situation the unconscious phantasies which accompanied the act of feeding, digesting, defecating etc. may come to be associated with, and affect, the act of taking in knowledge from the teacher.
- In order to learn, the pupil has at some point to experience his lack of knowledge, his need for it, or his 'hunger' for it. The pupil may be unable to bear this feeling of 'not knowing' and of being dependent on the teacher. The teacher possesses the desired knowledge and enjoys the benefits while the pupil is diminished by comparison.

- Certain pupils may have developed **negative unconscious phantasies** around the early experience of feeding. Through association, the dependency on the teacher for the 'nourishment' of knowledge may, for example, arouse feelings of intense envy which originate in the unconscious phantasy.

> ***Food for Thought***
>
> *In the language of everyday life, food and feeding are common metaphors or symbols for knowledge, thought, learning and mental processes generally. 'Food for thought', certain experiences being 'Hard to swallow', 'Biting off more than you can chew', 'I'm sick of it', 'I can't stomach it'.'Chewing something over', ideas being 'Difficult to digest', 'Hungry for knowledge', There are many more.*

- The pupil may **defend** against the envious, angry feelings by '**rubbishing**' overtly what the teacher has to offer or deprive the envied teacher the satisfaction of seeing the good which her knowledge or skill can bring to the pupil. Rather than experience her as a source of nourishment and therefore an object of envy, he protects himself from the feelings of belittlement or 'not having' or 'not knowing' by perceiving what she has to offer as worthless.

- A pupil who experiences the teacher in this way may characteristically have the unconscious phantasy of being able to 'feed' himself and therefore not need to take in any learning from the teacher. Such a child may leave the teacher **feeling de-skilled**, with nothing to offer. When a teacher systematically feels this kind of disparagement despite having real skills, there is a very good chance that **envy** is at work here. Indeed, the pupil is somehow communicating to the teacher by making her feel the unbearable feelings which he experiences in the learning situation. The teacher feels she has nothing to offer, that her skills are just not 'up to the mark', that she does not know what to do here. Ironically, the better the teacher, the more they may actually feel this. The pupil would not experience the impulse to spoil had he not perceived that there was something 'good' there to envy in the first place.

- Other pupils while not openly 'rubbishing' what the teacher has to offer may nevertheless **fail to make progress**. Envy may also be at work here. The pupil cannot take the risk of giving the teacher the pleasure of seeing him make use of what she has to offer. If she cannot enjoy what she has to offer, the pupil need not feel envious of her ability to 'feed' him knowledge.

- The pupil's own experience of envy can be so intense and anxiety-provoking due to the unconscious association with infantile experience, that he may defend against the envy he may himself provoke in others if he is successful. **Fear of others' envy** can also hinder the pupil's learning progress and contribute to chronic under-achievement.

- In extreme cases where a negative unconscious phantasy influences the perceptions of the pupil in the learning situation, the child may not be able to take in anything good from the learning experience. This pupil might need intensive therapeutic help.

3. The effect of emotional deprivation and loss in the learning situation (Bowlby)

It has been objected by some psychoanalytical theorists (Bowlby et al.) that the psychoanalytical perspective on child development places the emphasis almost exclusively on the content of the phantasy life of the child while denying the extent and influence of real life events on the development and the origin of maladaptive responses. However, the frame of reference when looking at the effects of deprivation of primary care or loss on the cognitive and emotional development of the child remains that of psychoanalysis (including the use of ego defences).

i) Attachment Theory and emotional deprivation and loss

- Clinical observations of the universal characteristics of the behaviour of infants when they became separated from their mother (or permanent primary care-giver) provided the basis for **attachment theory**.

- There is a critical time in very early infancy when babies formed a **bond with their primary care-giver** (parent or permanent parent substitute). This bond is termed **'attachment'**.

- Attachment is observable when the baby behaves in a way which is designed to bring the primary care-giver or **attachment figure** to them (searching for eye-contact, crying etc.).When babies are older, this attachment manifests itself in behaviour which tends to direct the baby towards the care-giver (reaching out, running towards, clinging etc.). These behaviours are called **attachment behaviours**.

- When babies are separated from their attachment figure they manifest behaviour which is called **separation anxiety**. This anxiety is experienced when attachment behaviour is activated (e.g. the attachment figure leaves the baby behind with a stranger or alone, or baby experiences fear and mother is not actually present etc.) but cannot be shut off or terminated (e.g. when the attachment figure is not immediately available).

- The aim of attachment behaviour is to seek the presence of the attachment figure and the **assuaging of the anxiety** which the separation aroused.

ii) Secure attachment

- When the attachment figure is able to respond appropriately to the infant's attachment behaviour, the infant's anxiety is relieved or assuaged. **Responding appropriately** might include actual holding or cuddling of the infant when they need to be reassured or comforted and doing this in a consistent way which arises from the **real needs of the child**.
- The infant comes to learn that he has a **reliable attachment figure** who is available for him and whose actions have a certain amount of predictability. The infant builds a picture of meaningful behaviour with trusted adults. Secure attachment gives the child what is called a '**secure base**'.
- If the infant has a secure base he is freed to go on to develop behaviours such as exploration of the environment. This particular behaviour is essential if the **learning potential** of the child is to have a chance of fulfilment.
- Through his interactions with the attachment figure, the infant develops what is termed an '**internal working model**'.
- In the case of secure attachment this internal working model equips the child with a picture of himself as a worthwhile individual. This 'worthwhileness' has been demonstrated by the **continual and affirming interaction** between himself and the attachment figure.

iii) Insecure attachment or loss of an attachment figure

- An infant might come to develop an insecure or anxious attachment when the attachment figure is **not emotionally available** to him significantly or repeatedly. (Extreme examples of this might be when the attachment figure is chronically depressed, ill or intensely preoccupied by inner or outer experiences).
- When the attachment figure is unable, for whatever reason, to respond appropriately to the infant's attachment behaviour, the child develops an internal working model of **self-doubt** and **depreciation**.
- He is unable to build up an experience of **consistent or meaningful relationships**. He may not feel safe enough to express negative feelings towards the attachment figure e.g. anger, frustration.
- These feelings may through the process of **defence mechanisms** (see above) be displaced onto significant others (e.g. teachers).
- Responding appropriately does not only mean giving the infant reassurance when he needs it. It can be just as **inappropriate** to give the infant so much reassurance that he never has the opportunity to learn to deal gradually with the inevitable frustrations of real life. He may be **over-protected.**

- In the case of insecure attachment, there is no secure base from which to explore the world around them and he is **less likely to achieve his full potential** in the learning situation.

- When a child suffers a **permanent loss** of an attachment figure through death or family break-up, their ability to manage and achieve the reorganisation of the personality which is necessary to adapt to the situation will be easier in the case of a child who has had the experience of secure attachment rather than insecure attachment.

iv) Implications of attachment theory in the learning situation

- Securely attached children are better able to take the risk of exploring new 'territory'. This is a necessary condition for the acquisition of new knowledge and skills.

- Children with a positive experience of attachment will more readily make positive new attachments e.g. to their teacher(s).

- Expectations of interaction with adults are positive and affirming of their own worth. They are more likely to be able to form stable and caring relationships with adults and to elicit positive and caring responses from them. They will be able to seek help when they are experiencing difficulty in the academic or social context in the classroom as their early experience of vulnerability is one of sensitive adult response to their need. They will possess a greater capacity for tolerating the inevitable frustrations of the process of learning. They will not feel threatened at having to share the attention of these adults with peers. Not being preoccupied with unresolved attachment problems, they are free to concentrate on the learning task and have a better chance of reaching their full potential.

- The converse is true to a greater or lesser degree in children who have formed insecure attachments.

- Intervention in the case of children whose emotional difficulties may stem from insecure attachment are based on attempts to modify the **internal working model** which the child carries with him. The more negative messages the child carries about himself, the more that child needs positive messages from significant others (class teachers among them) to alter these perceptions. Interventions based on the aim of raising the pupil's **self-esteem** and providing **clear boundaries** which offer an experience of **consistent interaction** are appropriate in this context.

v) Examples of insecure attachment in the learning situation

- **School phobia** has been linked to the existence of insecure attachment. Concerns for the well-being of the attachment figure in their absence or the lack of a secure emotional base may make the child anxious when he has to leave the attachment figure. This child may be incapable of making positive new attachments to his teacher. (The example of John also illustrates insecure attachment. His behaviour when mother left him in school on the first day back could be seen as a manifestation of separation anxiety.)

- There are aspects of the learning situation which can be experienced in an unconsciously symbolic way as linked to the **fear of abandonment** and activating similar responses. For example, when children do form attachments to the teacher, the imminent 'loss' of that teacher as at transition times from class to class or school to school or even during breaks in the school year can raise anxiety in children whose original attachment figure is/was unable to provide a secure attachment or base.
- **Beginnings and endings** can be particularly charged with difficulty for pupils with emotional and behavioural difficulties. On a large scale, beginning a new academic year or ending an old one can raise anxiety around e.g. 'not knowing' or of being 'abandoned'. How these events are approached can make a significant difference to these pupils.
- If a child is carrying an internal working model of self-doubt and depreciation, he may unconsciously set out to prove that this is the 'right' model each time he meets with new people, for example, teachers. This child may provoke negative reactions in the teacher and thus reinforce these feelings of self-doubt and worthlessness.

End of Term Blues

The practice of not telling pupils until the very last week or day who will be teaching them next year or the 'pulling apart' of the classroom on the last week can have a particular resonance for these pupils.

Most teachers will be aware of the atmosphere of the end of term and how traditionally we 'brace ourselves' for the unusual level of disruption which occurs at these times. On a lesser scale, the beginning and end of the school week can also be charged. Thought needs to be given to how the learning situation needs to be modified to contain the potential anxiety around these specific events.

4. Transference and Counter-transference in the learning situation (Freud)

i) Definition of Transference

- Transference is the psychoanalytical term used to describe the phenomenon whereby the client in analysis unconsciously endows the analyst with characteristics belonging to significant persons from the client's past.
- Transference occurs in relationships with other important figures in the person's life. A pupil may well bring transference into the relationship with the teacher.
- Transference may be **positive** (where the person is endowed with attributes of a significant past figure which the individual has experienced as positive) or **negative** (where the person is endowed with attributes which the individual has experienced as negative)
- When Freud first encountered this with his own patients, he regarded it as an impediment to the business of helping the patient. He believed it prevented the patient from being objective. However, he came to realise that it provided the analyst with invaluable information about the state of the patient's relationships with important early figures in their life and about how the patient perceived himself in this relationship. It gave important clues about the patient's present behaviour. By interpreting these reproduced or 'transferred' behaviours and beliefs the analyst could assist him to become aware of the 'leftover emotions' from this past relationship which continued to cause the patient problems in his adult life. He might do this by alerting the patient when he was behaving 'as if' the analyst were the patient's father or mother or other significant other.

  If, for example, the patient had a troubled relationship with a parent or parental figure which involved the patient feeling humiliated or in awe of the parent, he might unconsciously try to manipulate the analyst into behaving towards him in a way which reproduced these feelings. The analyst when aware of this could then, by refusing to enter the 'role', provide a neutral or objective ground where the patient could examine the origin of the feelings. Transference could be positive or negative. The analysts could be endowed with healthy characteristics from the client's past relationships and not just those which caused the client emotional pain.

ii) Definition of counter-transference

- Transference can be seen as a **'two-way' phenomenon**. In the same way as the client may bring transference to the figure of the analyst, so can the analysts bring elements of their own transference to the client.
- The analysts' **awareness of their own transference** in the situation can avoid a **distortion** of their perception of what is occurring in the transference relationship with the client.

'Here we go again!'

A common behaviour with pupils who have emotional or behavioural difficulties is seen in what teachers often call 'testing-out'. This might be seen to originate in the pupil's past experience of relationships with significant people. For example, the pupil who has experienced rejection may not at first respond to a teacher's attempts to form a positive relationship with them. Instead, these pupils may go through a period of testing out where they stand with the teacher. Such pupils may in effect be trying to bring about positive responses from the teacher and their testing-out behaviour needs to be seen in this light. It is as if the pupil is wondering if this teacher is 'just like all the other adults'. If the pupil has been emotionally hurt by adults in the past, he needs to 'test-out' whether this adult will repeat that interaction.

iii) Examples of transference and counter-transference in the learning situation

- In the case of **negative transference of a certain pupil onto the teacher**, the latter may feel that she is the repository for feelings which she has consciously done nothing to provoke. It could be argued, of course, that there are some objective characteristics of the teacher which are more likely to provoke both positive and negative transference. For example a teacher with a more authoritarian approach could trigger a negative transference derived from the pupil's relationship with an authoritarian parental figure. Even if the teacher does not then behave as the other figure did, the pupil might anticipate that she will and endow the teacher with intentions which are not objectively true. A teacher who establishes clear and firm boundaries may be expected by the pupil to behave in a tyrannical or unfair way as the pupil's parental figure may have done.

- Transference, insofar as it projects unconscious feelings or intentions on to the other, can also be used as an **ego defence**. This may result in a **projection** on to the teacher of feelings which the pupil might be finding unbearable. Earlier in the chapter we indicated that the way a teacher may be made to feel by certain pupils can provide information about what might be happening in emotional terms for the pupil. For example, a pupil who repeatedly makes a teacher feel de-skilled, hopeless, furious or confused etc. may be using the transference to 'put into' the teacher feelings which the pupil experiences in the learning situation which arouse anxiety and are alleviated by making the teacher feel them in his place. This could be seen in some ways as an unconscious attempt on the part of the pupil to communicate these unbearable feelings to the teacher. It is as if the pupil has an unconscious belief that if the teacher 'knows' how the pupil is feeling then she will be in a better position to cater for his emotional needs.

- The transference of some pupils may set up in teachers interactions which are to do with the experiences of the teacher's own past and these become enmeshed in the relationship with the pupil (counter-transference). Caution has to be exercised when attributing certain feelings to the pupil which may have more to do with the teacher's own experience. Open discussion in a supportive climate with qualified and experienced professionals may help to clarify this for the teacher.

Standing Back From It All

There is an intensity of feeling and a kind of 'predictability' about the interactions between the pupil and the teacher in the transference that is a good indicator that this is what is happening. It may be very hard for the teacher to resist falling into the trap of behaving towards the pupil in a certain way; the way he is unconsciously manipulating her to behave. Take, for example, the phenomenon of losing one's temper with a certain pupil continually and despite one's better professional judgement. Somehow we find ourselves doing it again and again even when we suspect that this is the aim (conscious or not) of the pupil (who will then sit back and enjoy it). This is a fairly banal but common example of how transference might be at work. It may indicate that the pupil has feelings of unbearable frustration and anger under the cover of bored or insolent indifference and he is projecting these feelings onto the teacher, literally making her feel them. The value of looking at the interaction in this way is that it may enable the teacher to stand back.

Instead of being 'fooled' by the pupils overt behaviour, the teacher may be able to look at the elements in the learning situation which may be arousing his frustration and anger. Is the pupil covering up real difficulties with learning? Does the pupil feel that his self-esteem is at risk? Does he feel that his needs are not being met? By asking questions about what might lie behind the behaviour we may be able to shift the dynamics of the interaction. Discussing with other colleagues, in a supportive climate, how a particular pupil makes the teacher feel can help to throw some light on what is occurring. It may be that the pupil has the same effect on the colleague or the colleague has had similar feelings about other pupils. The teacher may also bring transference into the relationship with the pupil too.

Summary of aspects of the psychoanalytical perspective as applied to the learning situation

- The **origin** of present emotional and behavioural difficulties in the learning situation derives from **significant past experience** often linked to those of early infancy

- The pupil is **not consciously aware** that the perceptions he or she bring to the present learning situation have their origin in significant past or early experience

- The behaviour of the pupil in the present learning situation can be seen as a **metaphor for the inner reality** of the pupil, based on unconscious beliefs about the nature of the self, and of relationships, formed through past experience

- The manifest behaviour is **meaningful** when seen as an unconscious attempt on the part of the pupil to avoid painful feelings or anxiety which are experienced as threatening to the pupil's sense of identity or self-worth

- The defence against psychic pain or anxiety may result in a **maladaptive response** to the demands of the learning situation

- **Interventions** are based on an assessment of the pupils emotional and behavioural difficulties which attempt to arrive at an awareness of the **possible unconscious meaning** which the pupil might be using to interpret the present situation

- The pupil may unconsciously bring to the relationship with the teacher(s) elements of significant past relationships which are then said to form the basis for a **transference**. The teacher may also unconsciously bring similar elements from her own past relationships to the relationship with the pupil (**counter-transference**)

- The pupil may communicate their emotional state to the teacher/carer through the unconscious process of **projection** whereby the teacher is made to feel the psychic pain which is unbearable to the pupil

As in all manifestations of problematic behaviour, there exists a continuum and **principles of prevention** are relevant here. By that we mean that even where the classroom practitioner is not trained to intervene, an understanding of the dynamics of the learning situation from the point of view of the unconscious meaning these children may bring to it can help the practitioner and the institution in which he or she operates. Teachers can begin to reflect on certain practices which may unwittingly exacerbate the difficulties of these pupils and by the same token, which practices, if they were to be adopted might contribute to an easing of the situation.

'Hope Springs Internal!'

Given that our pupils come to us with inner working models and habitual defensive responses to the experiences they have built up already, they may be more or less well-equipped to deal with the many demands of the learning situation and the anxieties which these may arouse at an unconscious level, some of which we have explored in the chapter.

Some pupils will have failed to resolve unconscious conflict effectively and are still enmeshed in the emotional difficulties this has caused and continues to cause. The attention which should be available for learning is therefore tied-up with these pre-occupations. These pupils have special educational needs which, until they are addressed, will continue to interfere with their access to and progress through the learning situation which reflects their true ability. When these needs are addressed successfully, the emotional energy or attention, hitherto taken up by the unconscious emotional conflict or anxiety is released and the pupil is enabled to direct this towards making progress in the learning situation.

By providing a secure environment which is responsive to the emotional needs of these pupils schools can help. Success in the learning situation, though sometimes very hard won for these pupils and their teachers, can strengthen the pupil's capacity to overcome difficulties and the resulting increase in self-worth and ability to adapt can have far-reaching effects.

Our tendency as teachers is to become overwhelmed by the emotional trauma and deprivation which we know some of our pupils experience on a day- to-day basis outside school. However, each new encounter with a significant other (e.g. a teacher) is an opportunity to re-work the inner model or modify the defence.

Through an awareness of how the learning task might be experienced as anxiety-provoking for all pupils, not just those with emotional and behavioural difficulties, schools can take measures to provide a secure and emotionally (and physically) unthreatening environment. This can go some way towards enabling the ego to perform its integrating and healing function, without, in the case of the less damaged or 'troubled' ego, recourse to specialist therapeutic intervention.

ASSESSMENT FROM THE PSYCHODYNAMIC PERSPECTIVE IN THE LEARNING SITUATION

In the following section and the later section on interventions, it needs to be stressed that although techniques are described, **it is not recommended that teachers apply these in the learning situation without receiving training in their use**. There are suggestions for preventative measures which can be and are used in schools where the pastoral and special educational needs practice is effective.

The difficulty of assessment in the learning situation from the psychodynamic perspective is that we are looking at unconscious conflicts and phantasies. For example, the ego defences which are being used to attempt to manage or resolve emotional conflicts are by definition resistant to being 'uncovered' or, because unconscious, are not ordinarily 'available' for examination in the ordinary context of the classroom.

i) Focus of assessment

Assessment from this perspective might attempt to discover:

- aspects of the learning situation which are experienced at an unconscious level with anxiety and the defences the pupil might be using in relation to them
- unconscious phantasies operating in the learning situation which affect the pupil's interactions in the learning situation
- the kind of relationships which pupil might unconsciously expect or 'look for' and what cues the pupil might be giving with respect to those relationships:
- unconscious internal working models of the self which affect the pupil's management of the dynamics of the learning situation

ii) Techniques of assessment

- Observation of the way the pupil responds when presented with a learning task. For example the pupil's:

  approach to the task (confidently, eagerly, anxiously etc)

  concentration span

  ability to persevere

  reaction to making mistakes

  appropriate use of teacher support

- **Learning profiles** and **records of attainment** are necessary to supplement the information gathered and to highlight any specific learning difficulties which would need to be addressed. The assessment can also be supplemented from the techniques discussed in the **behavioural, cognitive and ecosystemic perspectives**.
- **Projective techniques**: These are devices where the individual is presented with a set of stimuli (pictures, stories etc) and requested to respond to them in as unrestricted a manner as possible:

Examples:

Thematic Apperception Test which provides a means of revealing the pupil's needs, desires, beliefs and attitudes. These may in some cases be conscious but may remain unarticulated without the opportunity to project them onto ambiguous stimuli. The individual is given a series of black and white pictures which can be interpreted in a number of ways and is asked to tell a story about each.

Goodenough Draw a Person Test where the child is invited to draw the best picture of a person he or she can. Although this is primarily used as an intelligence test, and is therefore cognitive, it can be informative of the child's unconscious images of the self.

The Rorschach Psychodiagnostic Inkblot Test (1921) This is a test in which an individual is asked to interpret ten cards which are designed in the form of symmetrical inkblots, varying in colour and complexity.

The individual is required to say what immediately springs to mind and what there is specifically about the inkblot that leads to that response.

The aim of the test is to reveal an individual's unconscious conflicts. This happens through the individual projecting onto the inkblot underlying conflicts. The test itself comes with a manual for scoring the responses.

As with other projective tests there are concerns about low validity and reliability relating to the issues of subjective scoring. However, they are still found useful by practitioners as a rich source of information.

- **Family interviews** – where the history of the pupil's development and significant events are related. From observing the dynamics between the pupil and other family members inferences can be made about the 'role' the pupil might be playing within the family dynamic.

- **Kinetic Family Drawing** – where the pupil is asked to draw a picture of himself and his family. Inferences can be made here, for example, from where the child positions the different figures in the family in relation to himself and the colours, proportions, scale etc. (or lack of them).

- Discussion with teachers about the way the pupil's interactions with them affect them in emotional terms. Where **transference** might exist this can provide insight into the pupil's emotional difficulties and how they manifest in the learning situation particularly in the inter-action between teacher and pupil.

My Mum is Brilliant.
I go out with her to get shopping.

INTERVENTIONS FROM THE PSYCHODYNAMIC PERSPECTIVE IN THE LEARNING SITUATION

Principles of Specialist Intervention

Four key principles of Specialist Intervention are:

- Where the assessment indicates an intensive psychotherapeutic intervention with a trained child psychotherapist, defences and unconscious phantasies would be interpreted and the transference relationship encouraged. This professional may opt to have no direct links with the class teacher as this might be deemed to interfere with the effectiveness of the treatment in terms of boundaries and confidentiality.

- The assessment might indicate other forms of specialist support which may take place within the school context. These may depend on resources available in both human and material terms. They may be combinations of withdrawal of the pupil and support to the class/subject teacher and parents.

- Insight which the specialist and the class/subject teacher and the parents may have gained can be shared in an effort to address the pupil's needs in as effective a way as possible.

- Confidentiality of the work the pupil may undertake with the specialist in the withdrawal situation is important. But in good practice the summative information gained about the pupil's emotional difficulties can be shared in an attempt to meet the pupil's special educational needs.

Two examples of Specialist Intervention Technique

There are a number of effective specialist interventions to be found, though not widely, in schools e.g. educational therapy, art therapy, music therapy etc. The scope of this volume does not permit detailed analysis of these, however we have chosen to focus below on two specific techniques which a specialist teacher (as opposed to a psychotherapist) might use in work was being undertaken with the pupil.

i) Using the Metaphor - 'Working at one remove'

Although the assessment may have indicated the existence of ego defences, unlike the psychotherapist, the specialist teacher would not be interpreting these with the pupil. The anxiety this interpretation might raise could be damaging to the emotional well-being of the pupil unless the person had received extensive training. The specialist teacher would employ a method known as working through the metaphor or 'working at one remove'.

This method relies on the belief that the pupil, through a process of identification with e.g. the characters in a story he has read or has written, or the pictures he has drawn etc., is enabled to think about the feelings he may be bringing to the learning situation and gain some insight into how these may be hindering him. For example, if the pupil has told a story, the specialist teacher may ask '*How do you think the character in the story is feeling?*' and not '*I think you feel……when……*'. It is believed that, by sharing in a trusting relationship, the attribution of feelings or intentions to the character in the story or drawing, the pupil, through identification with the character, might be offered an opportunity to process and gradually come to terms with his own feelings without raising the anxiety which would accompany the experience of doing so directly.

ii) Voicing the feelings

This is still working 'at one remove' but does come closer to the pupil's direct experience than using the metaphor. Sometimes the emotional pain attached to certain experiences is such that he pupil is unable to think clearly about this. He may find it impossible to articulate the feelings even if he wanted to do so. The pupil may be helped to achieve an understanding of these feelings if they are voiced by the professional. However, caution must be exercised here too. For example, in the case of Carl (see the case study below), his feelings of guilt over his sister's accident were 'unspeakable'. He had in fact not even ventured the information to the school at any point nor his mother did not mention it. She confirmed the event when the specialist teacher asked about it but did not feel that Carl had been adversely affected by it. However in one of the early sessions with the specialist teacher, Carl went into great detail about this episode. The specialist teacher discussed this in supervision and felt that Carl had experienced enough safety with her to mention it in the first place. Referring back to this in later session when Carl was discussing his difficulty in concentrating in some lessons, the specialist teacher was able to voice the feelings which she thought Carl might be experiencing around this past episode and which may have been continuing to cause difficulty in the learning situation. In some ways she could be said to have '*spoken the unspeakable*' for Carl. By being very careful to avoid definitive sounding 'explanations' or, when referring directly to him, using words like 'might be feeling' and not '*are feeling*' the teacher left Carl free to make use of this or not.

Preventative Measures in Schools

The emphasis in this section is on **prevention**. As we indicated at the beginning of the chapter direct intervention with these pupils, especially those with extreme emotional and behavioural difficulties, may remain within the domain of the specialist. Schools need to identify which agencies can provide support in meeting the special educational needs of these pupils.

- **Whole-school practices**

Pupils with emotional and behavioural difficulties require an environment which actively seeks to reduce the incidence of potential or real anxiety and the related learning difficulties which these pupils might experience. A learning environment which offers security, consistency, clear boundaries (in terms of roles and responsibilities) and respect for individual differences can go a long way towards achieving this for a large number of pupils, including those who do not have identified emotional or behavioural difficulties. Behaving consistently, providing tasks which are set at the appropriate level for the pupil and providing clear instructions and realistic learning goals can help.

Schools can also encourage an active pastoral curriculum which recognises the needs of the whole child not just the academic, in particular the need for raising and maintaining self-esteem.

Schools might also want to consider how it will support staff through training in the area of emotional and behavioural difficulties. Training in child protection would be an important consideration in this context. Active partnership with parents will also be essential if the needs of pupils with emotional and behavioural difficulties are to be met.

- **Metaphor in the curriculum**

All pupils, not only those with emotional and behavioural difficulties, can be helped to explore their feelings, and the confusion which sometimes accompanies these, by use of appropriate stories or topics within the normal curriculum. The identification with characters, real or imaginary, can enable them to experience 'at one remove' similar conflicts and dramas in which they might find themselves. They may do this through discussion in class or creative writing or drama activities. (Although there are some books which focus specifically on feelings, most good children's books can be used in this way). All goo children's stories contain aspects of the struggle to overcome difficulties, to grow to a new understanding of the world and others and, ultimately, to accept our limitations in allowing ourselves to be who we are, 'warts and alls'. As teachers, we know and return constantly to these stories with our pupils.

- **Maintaining Boundaries**

Pupils need to feel that their teachers are sincere when they communicate with them and that they are concerned and involved in their well-being. However teachers should be alert to becoming enmeshed in their pupils' problems.

A non-judgmental approach to the pupil is necessary to avoid the pupil feeling that he is worthless as a person. But this does not mean that teachers should be indulgent or collusive. The pupil who feels his points of view are listened to by the teacher is more likely to develop a positive relationship with that teacher. However, the teacher needs to be aware that empathising with the pupil may result in over-identification with him or with the teacher projecting their own problems onto the pupil. These boundaries are important as emotional stress in the teacher can result. Being in touch with the painful feelings of the pupil may trigger the teacher's own painful feelings.

A case study using the Psychodynamic Perspective

Introduction

The following case study has been chosen as it illustrates how an intervention can use a variety of approaches (behavioural and psychodynamic). Although the behaviour of the pupil in question was not extremely disturbed, it nevertheless required support in exploring the underlying meaning of his behaviour in order to bring about change. It gives the reader a clearer idea of the kind of strategies that a psychodynamic approach might use in the school context. The period of this case study covered a term and a half from referral to evaluation and closure.

Referral

Carl was a pupil in NC Year 8. He was referred to the SEN Support Service as a result of repeated incidents of hostility and unco-operative behaviour towards teaching staff. He had been excluded for three days for verbally abusing a teacher. On his return he was sullen and the referral to the outside agency had a preventative aim. His referral was allocated to a teacher with specialist training in emotional and behavioural difficulties.

Assessment

Secondary Assessment Profile: (see the Behavioural Chapter) showed that Carl's hostility was directed at male members of staff. His achievement was below average to average in all subjects. The most prominent area of discrepancy between subject teachers' report was in the area of 11) Attitude towards self. Whereas most teachers scored him as between 3 and 4, a significant number of male teachers scored him between 1 and 2 and underlined the 'over-confident' and 'self satisfied' example words.

Pupil Interview: Carl mentioned that in his 6th year his younger sister had fallen from a first floor balcony resulting in head injuries which although not producing long-term damage had been cause for great concern at the time. It emerged that Carl felt in some way to blame for this event as he had been playing below with a football and felt he had perhaps been the attraction which caused his sister to climb onto the parapet. Carl believed that his sister's fall had held her up in terms of academic progress and that she would be doing much better in school if this had not happened. Carl had never discussed this incident with teachers in the school.

Parental interview: Carl was the oldest child. Carl's mother reported that she had separated from Carl's father when Carl was 9 years old. He had not seemed overly disturbed by the departure of father. Although still living in the same city, Carl had seen little of his father who was now running a successful business. He had experienced minor difficulties at Primary school with hostility towards certain members of staff. He seemed to her to be under-confident about his learning.

Formulation

- Carl's guilt about his sister's accident and his feeling of somehow being responsible resulted in an ambivalent attitude to his own academic achievement. He felt it was not fair that he was able and she was less so. This was holding him back in terms of achievement. There may have been an element of defence against his sister's envy.

- Since the departure of his father Carl had become the 'man around the house'. Partly, his anxiety might have been around being able to fulfil this role adequately and protect and provide for his family now and in the future. He had had to grow up faster than normally and had not a father upon whom to rely for guidance. Carl might have been denying the painful feelings around his father's leaving also as he seemed to shrug it off. Aspects of Carl's ambivalent feelings around his father were possibly being projected onto his male teachers. He may also have been displacing feelings of hostility towards his father onto his male teachers. He felt in competition with them and acted out a rather arrogant role in his relations with them. Perhaps, he needed to feel that he could be as grown up as them and as much in control. There was an element of their behaving towards him as a normal 13 year old which conflicted with the demands he put on himself to be a more adult father-figure in his family. His hostility and unco-operative moods and arrogance towards male teachers might be seen as him having to prove himself as much in control of things as them.

Intervention

- To carry out regular termly round-robins using the Secondary Assessment Profile with teachers and feedback progress, if any, to Carl. Select specific lessons in which to monitor Carl's progress on a weekly basis with behavioural targets and enable him to participate in self-assessment (Intervention drawn from the behavioural perspective)

- To see Carl on his own for 40 minutes/week to work therapeutically with Carl through a learning task. (Intervention drawn from the psychodynamic perspective).

Intervention Strategies

- **Behaviour Monitoring Book**: Using the information from the Secondary Assessment Profile, Carl and the teacher selected lessons where Carl experienced difficulties with the teachers which resulted in hostile or unco-operative behaviour and agreed on behaviour targets which Carl would try to maintain. These were reviewed each time Carl and the teacher met and were also reviewed by Year Head and Carl's mother.

- **Voicing the feelings**: When Carl spoke of his sister's accident, the teacher tried to put into words the muddle of feelings which Carl was obviously still experiencing around this event. She felt that since Carl had chosen to give her this information there may well have been a desire on his part to seek help with it. She did not dwell on it but remarked to Carl that 'Sometimes children feel that it's their fault when something awful happens to a person close to them even when they know it isn't. I wonder if you don't sometimes still feel that when you remember your sister falling.' Or again when it was appropriate, 'Sometimes when young people are worried about something it stops them from being able to get on with other important things, like learning in school.' or, 'Perhaps you might feel sometimes that it's not fair that you can read when your little sister finds it a bit hard'

  The teacher was careful not to say directly that this was what Carl was actually experiencing. It is as if she put it to him as an idea which he might find useful to consider. There is a subtle but important distinction between saying '*I wonder if...*' and '*you are obviously experiencing...*'; between '*perhaps...*' and '*What is happening here is...*' etc.

- **Using the Metaphor**: In one of the early sessions with Carl he spoke about a friend of his who had run away from home. Often what children chose to talk about in the beginning sessions has a great deal of symbolic importance. Teachers should be alert to this and try as much as possible to follow the 'clues' which children give them in seemingly random anecdote. The teacher wondered if this was not something which Carl rather wished he could do as it would lessen his immediate feelings of anxiety around having to live up to his self-imposed role of father substitute for the family as well as allowing him to experience the 'freedom' of the adult world which he did not experience as a Year 8 pupil in school. She did not make this suggestion to Carl or share her hypotheses with him. However, she proposed that Carl might like to imagine what this boy would be experiencing now and an activity developed where Carl, entering the role of the runaway himself, wrote a letter to a friend to let her know where he was and how he was surviving. This activity became a regular sort of 'soap-opera', with Carl writing letters to the friend and the friend replying (also written by Carl). In the first letter Carl was at pains to ensure that the friend informed his mother that he was alive and well but that he had things to do and that he would return when he had done them. Perhaps this served to liberate Carl from feelings of guilt over his mother's anxiety about his whereabouts. This released him to explore the fantasy to the full. The world into which Carl's friend had fallen was very like the world where Carl's father had a business. The friend triumphed over difficulties, became a successful business man and eventually returned to his mother's home to inform her that she was a grandmother!

The metaphor for the feelings Carl was exploring around making one's own way in the world and becoming an adequate father are obvious. However Carl was able to explore these feelings 'at one remove' through the metaphor which he had 'chosen' himself.

- **The Learning Task**: Carl wrote a large number of letters which he drafted and corrected and finally transferred to a word-processor. He became very eager to achieve a high standard of presentation. Ostensibly for Carl, when he met with the specialist teacher, the purpose, aside from reviewing actual behavioural progress in the targeted lessons, the activity was in essence no different to any writing activity i.e. it was curriculum focused. His success with this curricular activity contributed to raising his confidence about his ability in other areas in which he had previously been underachieving. He was pleased to share his finished collection with his English teacher.
- **Evaluation**: The behaviour monitoring book showed over the period of the term it was used that the incidence of Carl's hostile interactions with teachers was reduced and his behaviour became more co-operative. Carl's confidence in his ability to respond to the demands of the learning situation increased and round-robins showed that teachers were satisfied that he was beginning to achieve according to his ability. Carl himself suggested that he would be able to manage in school without the weekly sessions with the support teacher. After an agreed period of 'closure' the intervention ended.

EVALUATION FROM THE PSYCHODYNAMIC PERSPECTIVE

Evaluation from this perspective is based on inferences made by the therapist and/or specialist teacher in conjunction with the class/subject teachers, pupil and parents as to changes in the pupil's behaviour as regards:

- qualitative changes in the relationship of the pupil with teacher(s) and peers
- quality of engagement with the learning task
- level of the pupil's self-esteem.

This may involve looking at baseline observations and repeating them to measure change where possible. It may also involve using projective techniques as for the assessment. Learning profiles and levels of attainment could be used and again measured against those used at the assessment stage. Interviews with the family and with the child and teacher(s).

As with the other perspectives, on-going review is part of the evaluation, and re-formulation or re-assessment might be called for in certain cases. Depending on how troubled the pupil is at the start, and on how supportive his social and emotional environment is, more or less progress will be made. Often these children need continued support throughout their school career and beyond. Therapeutic work with the pupil's family can be crucial to the long-term effectiveness of any intervention.

Charts and Books

IT and SELF-ESTEEM

Monitoring books or behaviour charts are not new in concept, but since the advent of Desk Top Publishing facilities it has been possible to produce materials of a high quality which can be attractive to pupils. The use of such materials seems to increase interest in the intervention process itself as well as raising self-esteem. This can be done through :

- Use of POP images: these can selected by the pupil and scanned in or imported from existing collections of "clip art".
- Personalisation: the student's own name can be used – on the cover and within the text. One chart I made allowed Leonardo (one of the Ninja Mutant Turtles) to say *"Well Done, Darren, have another slice of pizza"*. Darren was delighted as he coloured in and pasted another slice of pizza onto his chart. As well as the Turtles, Bart Simpson among many others have been co-opted in support of good behaviour.
- Involvement in design: students can be involved in the contents and the design of the monitoring book or chart. They can select pictures / do drawings to be incorporated, as well as becoming involved in the using the actual production of the resource on the computer. All this can contribute to their sense of commitment to the project.

Counselling and Desk Top Publishing

In working individually with students, one can discuss with them what they like / don't like about school, what makes them angry / sad / happy etc. With younger students this will often involve some writing and picture drawing. It is then possible to turn these words and images into little books which can, if appropriate, be used by them as a reader. One year 11 pupil who was a non-reader 'wrote' and 'published' a 3000 word autobiographical account of his dyslexia.

Another useful format that has been used for raising self-esteem has been to work with pupils on developing their version of a book called 'My dad is Brilliant',

I don't like teachers bossing me about — including Don

extending it to include all appropriate parents, carers and guardians. Examples of pages have been included within the text of this book.

This kind of intervention is important for a number of other reasons including:

- The raising of pupils' self-esteem by them seeing a high quality, attractive product come out of their efforts
- The production of a 'permanent' reflection and a summary of their thoughts and feelings, both positive and negative, which reinforces their sense of self and individuality

Video

It is also possible to use video material produced by pupils (by linking up with a computer system) to illustrate the writing which perhaps developed out of an activity. The authors have effectively used this approach for such topics as: bullying and friendship.

MAKING CHARTS AND MONITORING BOOKS WORK

These kinds of interventions rarely work by themselves. They are opportunities to create success for a pupil and to engage their interest in the process. The following points should be born in mind when using interventions which involve Charts and Monitoring Books:

- **Commitment**: the teacher needs to be fully committed to making it work. In the short term it might require an extra input of work and effort. Teachers can sometimes feel that giving more attention to misbehaving students is unfair to class members and a burden on themselves. I think that the situation *is* improved because the teacher takes control of the situation by becoming proactive rather than being at the mercy of the pupil's misbehaviour. Secondly, it is an improvement because it is a planned stage in the longer-term goal of providing the child with a fair rather than an unfair amount of teacher attention.
- **Involvement**: through the IT methods described above / the use of a timer / marking their own chart / filling in their own monitoring book (self-assessment

or as a means of self-control) / colouring in / cut and paste (eg slices of pizza onto a base when certain levels of achievement have been obtained).

- **Keep it interesting** - Boredom can be a real problem. Even the most interesting chart or monitoring book can become tedious and a chore. Think of ways of varying the intervention by regularly changing or developing the idea. Use a chart for a couple of weeks; then use a book, then have a break; and so on. In the end, the "boredom factor" can help the process of weaning off regular and material means of recording progress.

- Descriptive targets using **SMART** criteria:

  Specific: *Jane is trying to sit in her seat and not wander around*, rather than *"Jane needs to get on with work more."* More specific still would be *"Jane is aiming not to get out of her seat more than 7 times a lesson"*. It is really only in practice that it can be seen how precise the targets need to achieve the desired changes. If it doesn't seem to work, change it.

  Measurable: A baseline of times out of seat needs to be established. Jane can then make an entry on her chart whenever she does get out of her seat. She might also have to indicate, from a range of possibilities, the reason why.

  Achievable: In order for Jane to succeed, the targets have to be (or at least seem to the pupil) achievable. If she is usually out of her seat 10 times in a lesson, then a target of no more than 7 times might be a practical target for the first week.

  Relevant: The out of seat behaviour needs to be seen as a problem. Maybe the real problem is hitting other children whilst wandering around the room; if the wandering is stopped, the hitting is less likely to happen.

  Time-limited: Time limits are only one way of making target-setting a finite project, In the example of the Docklands Railway, the limit was set by the length of the map used as a chart. More usually the limit might be, *"We'll be using this chart for the next two weeks"*, or *"This monitoring book will be used until half-term"*.

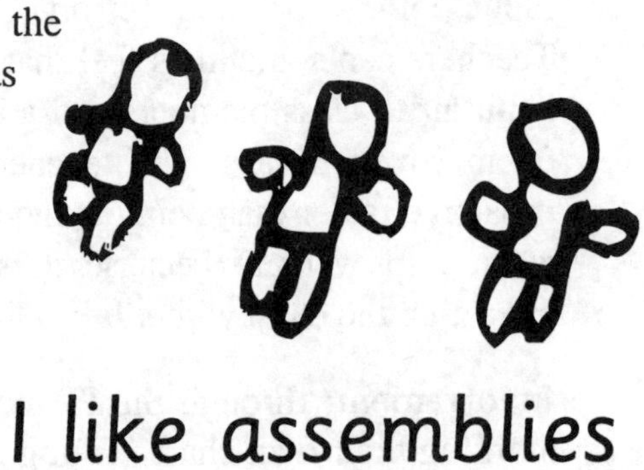

- **Success is important**. The intervention should be regarded as the opportunity to facilitate success. Everything should work towards it. Frequently, students with whom charts and monitoring books are used, not only have specific behaviour difficulties but also an underlying sense of being a person 'who can't change' or 'who can't succeed', (i.e. pupils who have an external locus of control).

- **Stand alone vs leading to reward**: Charts and Monitoring Books can be used alone and be rewarding merely because of their novelty factor and attractiveness. They can also be used as a means of recording progress towards a larger goal. For example, *'When you are able to stick enough slices of pizza on to complete it, your mum will take you down to Pizza Hut for a real one'*,

- **Teacher-monitoring vs pupil-monitoring**: The value of teacher-monitoring vs pupil-monitoring is discussed in the text. However, pupil-monitoring is less time consuming for the teacher and in a secondary school, it can avoid contributing to lines of pupils waiting to see a subject teacher at the end of a lesson.

- **Opportunity for discussion / review of behaviour**: A key aspect of using Charts and Monitoring Books is that they provide a positive focus for discussion about the behaviour. If targets are carefully set and there is good opportunity for improvement, it is then possible to congratulate a child for improving their behaviour, rather than complaining at them for not having stopped altogether. Teachers can fairly easily notice when a behaviour has stopped altogether; it is much harder for them (without monitoring) to notice when it is just an improvement that has been made. The chart can act as a tangible focus for pupils themselves to see progress. They can also counteract feelings of discouragement which both pupils and teachers can experience.

- **Attention-seeking and Attention-giving**: Charts and books can be used with 'attention-seeking' pupils as part of a process of reducing their apparent dependency on teacher attention. Charts, monitoring books as well as stickers and certificates can have the effect of 'radiating' teacher attention even when the teacher is not present. This is particularly so if the chart or sticker is the focus and vehicle for positive pupil-teacher contact. It is helpful to regard these activities as a means of making visible the progress a pupil is making as well as putting that progress under the control of the pupil. Pupils for whom these kinds of strategies are useful are those who:

    - Attempt to gain attention through illegitimate means
    - Have little sense of their own ability to succeed and to make visible progress

These kinds of strategies also enable teachers to acknowledge efforts and improvements where previously those same efforts may have gone unnoticed or even apparently warranted complaining about. They can provide hope where once there was only disappointment and discouragement – teachers' and pupils'.

Using charts with classes

Charts can be effectively used for class interventions, both at primary and secondary level. As with other charts, any reward or reinforcer needs to be based on when certain targets are achieved rather than if. The anxiety of if can often lead to failure.

Two primary school examples that have been used are:

The Helpful and Friendly Tree

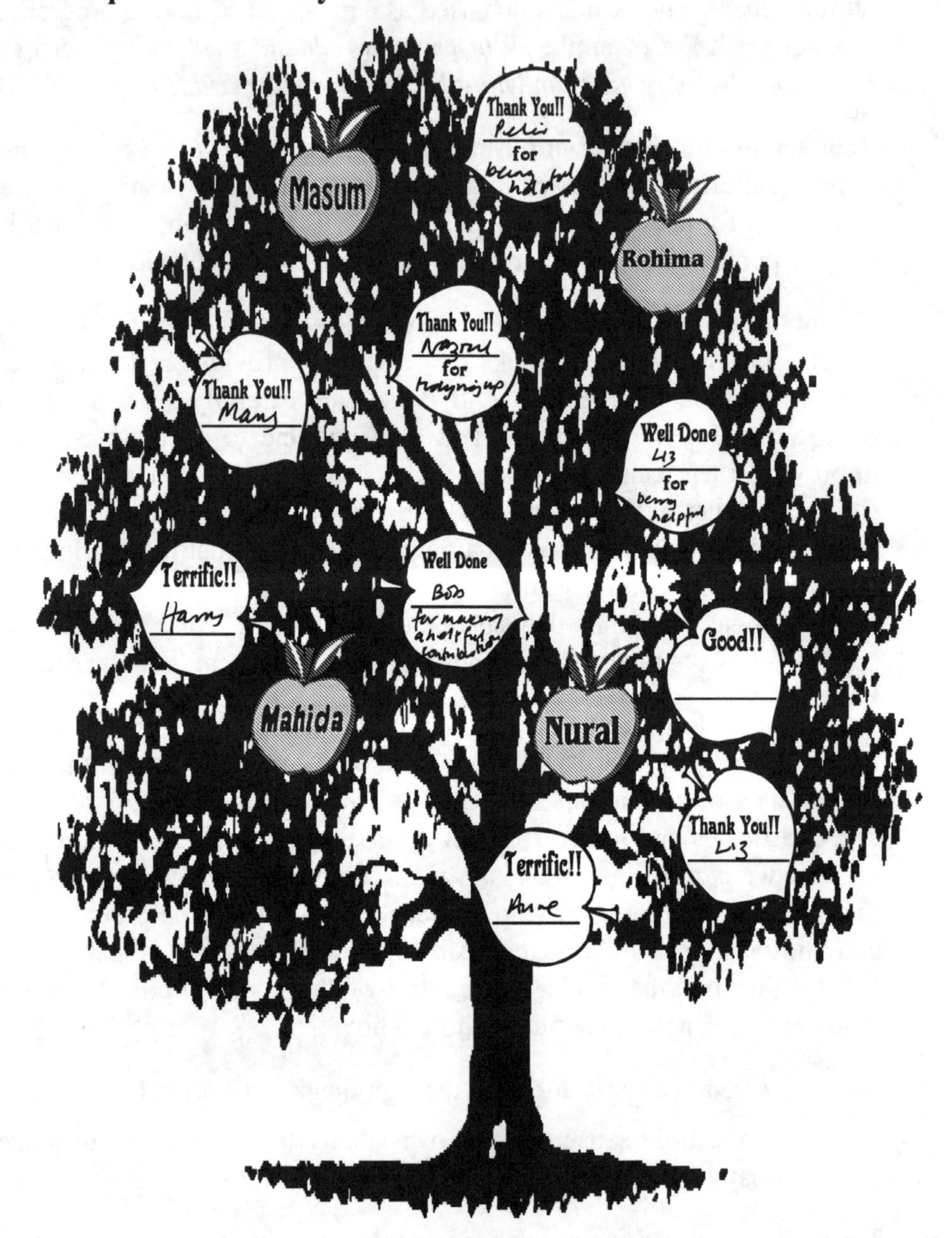

Skybluepink Class'
Helpful and Friendly Tree

On the classroom wall is a picture of a tree. They can be quite small – A3 perhaps right through to 3ft by 4ft depending on the space available and the profile you want it to receive. Specific targets are set and when class members achieve those targets they receive a leaf which might, for instance, have on it the words: *'Thank you __________ for being helpful'*. The space being filled in with the pupil's name. It would be awarded publicly at, for instance, carpet time and the pupil would stick it on the tree. When a pupil had received five leaves they would get an apple with their name on to stick on the tree. If different colours are used each week, it is possible to monitor the success rate.

A further development is to allow pupils to nominate class members who have been helpful or co-operative.

Similar strategies have been used successfully in secondary schools. As with all of these kinds of strategies, it is the commitment of the teacher which will make it work. If the teacher appears to take it seriously, then it is likely that the pupils will, although it must be true to say that the culture of the school can be more or less encouraging.

The emphasis of this kind of intervention should be on **making visible** acknowledgment of pupils' efforts, reinforcing their efforts to conform to the needs and norms of a class group.

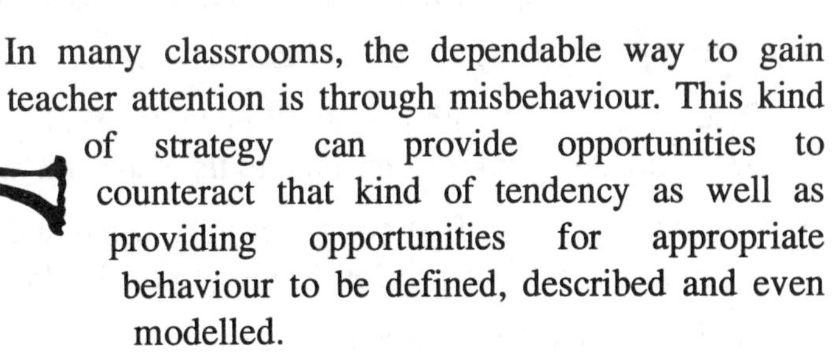

In many classrooms, the dependable way to gain teacher attention is through misbehaviour. This kind of strategy can provide opportunities to counteract that kind of tendency as well as providing opportunities for appropriate behaviour to be defined, described and even modelled.

The Docklands Railway

This intervention was used with a year 6 class who's teacher found it difficult to get them to read in silence. On the wall was a map of the Docklands Railway. The train moved along the railway from station to station as each day they spent longer and longer times engaged in silent reading. They started of at Tower Hill, and when they reached Stratford, going via Island Gardens, they were reading silently for ½ an hour at a time. The 'reward' was a trip on the Docklands Railway, from one end to the other, with a picnic lunch in Greenwich Park. Such rewards can easily be embedded in, or emerge from, the planned work of the class. This does not detract from their sense of specialness and their being a visible sign of the success of the pupils' efforts.

GUIDELINES FOR THE EFFECTIVE USE OF BEHAVIOUR CHARTS and MONITORING BOOKS

PRECONDITIONS

- Is this type of intervention appropriate with your pupil?
- Are the participants in agreement over their use?
- Can they be used in the given context?
- Are the parties committed to their use?
- Are they well-designed?

POINTS TO CONSIDER

Some of the things that make these interventions work are:

- It is necessary to observe the pupil to establish specific target behaviours: up to three. Start with one or two to begin with so as not to overload the pupil.
- Set up appropriate conditions to facilitate the success of the programme: consider teaching techniques, seating arrangements, level of work, sanctions, rewards etc.
- Inform participants of your programme and others who are affected.
- Discuss the chart with the pupil: encourage the pupil to take ownership of the chart by asking the pupil to contribute to its goals and design.
- Introduction of the first chart: consider when and how often it will be completed by yourself and the pupil and where it will be displayed.
- Praise the pupil accordingly. Consider the effects of the chart on other pupils and how the rest of the class can become involved.
- Keep appropriate people informed as to progress.
- Have a weekly / twice weekly review of the chart.

- Praise and discuss specific behaviour with the pupil.
- Reward desired behaviours frequently and immediately.
- Extend periods between filling up a chart.
- Consider what you will do if there is a lapse in the pupil's motivation.
- You may need to increase rewards or reassess the chart completely.
- Gradually introduce all the target behaviours, reviewing progress regularly, and the demands that it is placing on the participants and the class.
- Consider the effect the chart is having on the pupil's relationships with his or her peers.
- Begin to phase out the use of the chart when it has become clear that the target behaviours can be maintained without the need for the pupil to be on the chart.
- Remind yourself and others of the pupil's successful use of the chart.
- Having a small number of targets. 3 frequently seems a good number, but certainly no more than 5.
- Make the targets attainable. It may take some time to gauge the right level for the target. It has to provide an opportunity for success, not another means of confirming failure.
- 2 out of 3 targets might be pretty easy to achieve. The third one can be more difficult and might be considered the real target of the intervention. This way overall success is likely.
- Break it down into manageable time slots. In secondary school, break a day up into periods. In a primary school, before play, after play, after lunch etc. Use the book only in particular lessons, or only for certain portions of the day.
- Having a space for **positive comments** to be written, so as to increase the opportunities for positive interaction. It can form useful feedback to parents, although they may need priming on how to respond positively.
- Use self-monitoring or at least some pupil involvement in filling it in, perhaps underlining words or colouring stars, footballs et.
- If a continuum is used, 3 – 5 points is helpful in making some kind of success likely. Two examples are:

Steven sat on the carpet quietly:

Hardly at all **Some of the time** **Most of the time**

How much did Nazia contribute to class discussion:

Not at all **A little** **Sometimes** **Quite a lot** **A lot more than usual**

BIBLIOGRAPHY

GENERAL

Ayers, H., Clarke., D., Ross, A., and Bonathan, M., (1993) *Assessing Individual Needs: A Practical Approach*. London: David Fulton Publishers.

Bootzin, R., Acocella, J., Alloy, L., (1993) (Sixth Edition) *Abnormal Psychology: Current Perspectives*. London: McGraw-Hill Inc.

Cramer, D., (1992) *Personality and Psychotherapy: Theory, practice and research*. Milton Keynes: Open University Press.

Daniels, H. and Corrie, L., The Management of Discipline in Special Schools in *The Management of Behaviour in Schools,* Varma, V., (Editor) (1993). Longman.

Epanchin, B., and Paul, J., (1987) *Emotional Problems of Childhood and Adolescence: A Multidisciplinary Perspective*. Oxford: Maxwell Macmillan.

Eysenck, M.J., (1994) *Perspectives on Psychology*. Hove: Lawrence Eribaum Associates.

Hastings, N. and Schwieso, J., (1987) *New Directions in Educational Psychology: 2. Behaviour and Motivation in the Classroom*. London: Falmer Press.

Herbert, M., (1991) *Clinical Child Psychology: Social Learning, Development and Behaviour*. Chichester: Wiley.

Kazdin, A., (1988) *Child Psychotherapy: Developing and Identifying Effective Treatments*. London: Routledge

Kline, P., (1993) *Personality: The Psychometric View*. London: Routledge.

McLeod, J., (1993) *An Introduction to Counselling*. Buckingham: Open University Press.

Norwich, B., (1990) *Reappraising Special Needs Education*. London: Cassell.

Wenar, C., (1994) (Third Edition) *Developmental Psychopathology: From Infancy through Adolescence*. London: McGraw-Hill.

BEHAVIOURAL PERSPECTIVE

Herbert, M., (1981) (Second Edition) *Behavioural Treatment of Children With Problems: A Practice Manual*. London: Harcourt Brace Jovanovitch College Publishers.

Herbert, M., (1988) *Working With Children And their Families*. London: The British Psychological Society in association with Routledge.

Kazdin, A., (1994) *Behaviour Modification in Applied Settings*. Pacific Grove: Brooks/ Cole Publishers.

Skinner, B.F. (1993) *About Behaviorism*. London: Penguin.

Wheldall, K., Merrett, F., and Glynn, T., (1986) *Behaviour Analysis in Educational Psychology*: In Association with Positive Products. Beckenham: Croom Helm.

COGNITIVE PERSPECTIVE

Bandura, A., (1977) *Social Learning Theory*. Englewood Cliffs. N.J: Prentice-Hall.

Beck, A.T., (1989) *Cognitive Therapy and the Emotional Disorders*. London: Penguin.

Dobson, K.S. (Editor) (1988) *Handbook of Cognitive-Behavioural Therapies*. London: Hutchinson.

Ellis, A., (1962) *Reason and Emotion in Psychotherapy*. New York: Lyle, Stuart.

Feindler, E., Ecton, R., (1986) *Adolescent Anger Control: Cognitive-Behavioral Techniques*. Oxford: Pergamon.

Kendall, P.C. and Braswell, L., (Second Edition) (1993) *Cognitive-Behavioral Therapy for Impulsive Children*. London: Guilford Press.

Meichenbaum, D., (1977) *Cognitive-Behavior Modification*. New York: Plenum.

Trower, P., Casey, A., and Dryden, W., (1988) *Cognitive-Behavioural Counselling in Action*. London: SAGE Publications.

Walker, James E. and Shea, Thomas M. (1991) *Behavior Management*. Maxwell Macmillan Inernational Editions.

ECOSYSTEMIC PERSPECTIVE

Cooper, P., (1993) *Effective Schools for Disaffected Students*: Integration and Segregation. London: Routledge.

Cooper, P., Smith, C.J., and Upton, G., (1994) *Emotional & Behavioural Difficulties: Theory to Practice*. London: Routledge.

Dowling, E., and Osborne, E., (editors) (Second Edition (1994) *The Family & The School: A Joint Systems Approach to Problems with Children*. London: Routledge.

Molnar, A., and Lindquist, B., (1989) *Changing Problem Behaviour in Schools*, San Francisco: Jossey-Bass.

Street, E., and Dryden, W., (editors) (1988) *Family Therapy in Britain*, Milton Keynes: Open University Press.

PSYCHODYNAMIC PERSPECTIVE

Brown, Dennis and Pedder, (1979) Jonathan, *Introduction to Psychotherapy.* London: Routledge

Bettelheim, Bruno, (1991) *The Uses of Enchantment.* Harmondsworth: Penguin

Bowlby, John, (1978) *Attachment and Loss Volumes 1 – 3*. Harmondsworth:Penguin Education

Bowlby, John, (1979) *The Making and Breaking of Affectional Bonds.* London: Routledge

Freud, Sigmund, *The Theory of Psycholanalysis*. Harmondsworth: Penguin

Freud, Anna, (1966) *Normality and Pathology in Childhood.* London: Karnac

Freud, Anna, *The Ego and the Mechanisms of Defence*. London: Hogarth

Klein, Melanie, *Envy and Gratitude and other works 1946 – 63*. London: Virago

Rycroft, Charles, (1968) A *Critical Dictionary of Psychoanalysis.* Harmondsworth: Penguin

Winnicott, Donald, (1971) *Playing and Reality.* London: Tavistock / Routledge

Winnicott, Donald, (1991) *The Child, the Family and the Outside World.* Harmondsworth: Penguin

THE LEARNING SITUATION

Barrett, Muriel, and Trevitt, Jane, (1991) *Attachment Behaviour and the Schoolchild* London: Tavistock / Routledge

DfE, (1994) *Pupils with Problems.* HMSO

Caspari, Irene, (1976) *Troublesome Children in the Classroom.* London: Routledge

Fontana, David, (1981) *Psychology for Teachers.* Basingstoke: BPS Books, Macmillan

Greenhalgh, Paul, (1994) *Emotional Growth and Learning.* London: Routledge

Hanko, Gerda, (1991) *Special Needs in Ordinary Classrooms.* Oxford: Blackwell

Robertson, John, (1989) (Second Edition) *Effective Classroom Control.* London: Hodder & Stoughton

Rogers, Bill, (1994) *Behaviour Recovery.* Melbourne: ACER

Rogers, Bill, (1990) *You Know the Fair Rule.* Harlow: Longman

Rogers, Bill, (1990) *The Language of Discipline.* Plymouth: Northcote House Publishers

Rogers, Bill, (1990) *Supporting Teachers in the Workplace.* Queensland: Jacaranda Press

Saltzberger-Wittenberg, Esca, (1993) *The Emotional Experience of Teaching and Learning.* London: Routledge

COGNITIVE ASSESSMENT PUPIL QUESTIONNAIRE

This form can be used as a means of assessing a pupil's thoughts, attitudes, expectations and beliefs in the school context.

Circle appropriate number on each continuum and underline or add relevant words

Unless otherwise indicated: 1 = Poor 3 = OK 5 = Excellent

BEHAVIOUR:

What do you THINK about your behaviour in:

1) Classrooms *1 2 3 4 5* **2) Corridors** *1 2 3 4 5*

3) Assembly *1 2 3 4 5* **4) Toilets** *1 2 3 4 5*

5) Playground *1 2 3 4 5* **6) Outside school** *1 2 3 4 5*

7) How do you generally behave? *1 2 3 4 5*

Interfering Helpful Unhelpful Rude Polite Violent Friendly Talkative Loud Quiet Hardworking Lazy

8) What do you THINK about changing your behaviour?

1 2 3 4 5

Unable to change Maybe able to change Able to change

I don't have the power I do have the power I don't want to I want to

Teachers stop me Teachers will help me Pupils stop me Other pupils will help me

9) What do you think of yourself? *1 2 3 4 5*

Confident Lacking in confidence Attractive Unattractive Clever Stupid Interested Disinterested

10) In general, do you THINK teachers' behaviour towards you is:

1 2 3 4 5

Helpful Unhelpful Unfriendly Polite Rude Friendly Caring Aggressive Interested Not interested

In particular?

11) What do you THINK about the behaviour of other pupils towards:

YOURSELF: *1 2 3 4 5*

EACH OTHER: *1 2 3 4 5*

TEACHERS: *1 2 3 4 5*

12) What do you think of your school? *1 2 3 4 5*

Too small Just the right size Too big Poorly decorated Pleasantly decorated

Badly designed Too hot Too cold Badly lit Too noisy Too crowded

Designed by Don Clarke and Harry Ayers at the Support for Learning Service, Tower Hamlets
In '*Perspectives on Behaviour*' Published by David Fulton

WORK:

13) What do you THINK about the level of work?

1 = Too difficult *2 = Difficult* *3 = Just right* *4 = Easy* *5 = Too easy*

Mathematics	1 2 3 4 5		1 2 3 4 5
English	1 2 3 4 5		1 2 3 4 5
Science	1 2 3 4 5		1 2 3 4 5

14) What do THINK about the relevance of the work to you?

1 = None *2 = Little* *3 = Some* *4 = A lot* *5 = Completely*

Mathematics	1 2 3 4 5		1 2 3 4 5
English	1 2 3 4 5		1 2 3 4 5
Science	1 2 3 4 5		1 2 3 4 5

15) What do you THINK about your level of achievement?

1 = Poor *2 = Not very good* *3 = Average* *4 = Good* *5 = Very good*

Mathematics	1 2 3 4 5		1 2 3 4 5
English	1 2 3 4 5		1 2 3 4 5
Science	1 2 3 4 5		1 2 3 4 5

16) Do you THINK you can do better?

1 = Not at all *2 = Possibly* *3 = Some* *4 = Quite a lot* *5 = A lot*

Mathematics	1 2 3 4 5		1 2 3 4 5
English	1 2 3 4 5		1 2 3 4 5
Science	1 2 3 4 5		1 2 3 4 5

If I tried harder *If the work was made more interesting* *If I received more help* *If I brought the right equipment*

17) What do THINK about your effort?

1 = Poor *2 = Not very good* *3 = Average* *4 = Good* *5 = Very good*

Mathematics	1 2 3 4 5		1 2 3 4 5
English	1 2 3 4 5		1 2 3 4 5
Science	1 2 3 4 5		1 2 3 4 5

Any other comments?

Designed by Don Clarke and Harry Ayers at the Support for Learning Service, Tower Hamlets
In '*Perspectives on Behaviour*' Published by David Fulton

INTERVIEW SHEET for CARERS

Name: | **Age:** | **Date:**

School: | **Form / Class:**

This sheet is intended as a structure for interviewing carers about their thoughts and feelings with respect to the pupil.

1) Are they a problem to you? *Never* *Occassionally* *Sometimes* *A lot*

2) Where are they a problem? *At home* *In other peoples' homes* *In the street* *In shops* *In the park* *Public places* *Other*

3) What kind of problem(s)? *1 = Rarely* *2 = Occassionally* *3 = Regularly*

Attention-seeking	1	2	3	Bullying	1	2	3
Disobedient	1	2	3	Temper outburst	1	2	3
Depressed	1	2	3	Wetting / soiling	1	2	3
Verbally aggressive	1	2	3	Staying out late	1	2	3
Physically aggressive	1	2	3	Noisy	1	2	3
Argumentative	1	2	3	Other	1	2	3

4) What seems to lead to the problem(s)?

When asked to do something by an adult / child

When they want something material e.g. clothes or non-material e.g. attention

When someone comes to the home - an adult / child

When they are with their peer group

When limits / rules are imposed

Other

5) What do you do about the problem(s)?

Tell them off

Discuss the problem with them

Punish them

Bribe them

Encourage them to do better

Nothing in particular

Don't know waht to do

Other

Designed by Don Clarke and Harry Ayers In '*Perspectives on Behaviour*' Published by David Fulton

4) What punishments do you use?

How effective are they?

5) What rewards or encouragements do you use?

How effective are they?

6) In what ways would you like your child to change?

- Quieter
- More obedient
- Friendlier
- More polite
- More considerate
- Other
- More helpful
- Work harder at school
- Be more respectful
- Happier
- More relaxed

7) Do you expect your child to change?

YES / POSSIBLY / NO

What might make it difficult?

- Character or temperament
- Lack of social skills
- Bad influence of friends / peers
- Rejects help
- Other
- Lack of communication skills
- Poor learning skills
- Acts without thinking
- Don't know what to do
- Teachers / school pick on him / her

8) What are your general feelings about your child's problem?

- Anger
- Puzzlement
- Discouragement
- Powerlessness
- Other
- Sadness
- Hopelessness
- Frustration
- Irritation

ANALYSIS OF INTERACTIONS SHEET

Name: | **Age:** | **Date:**

Form / Class: | **NC Year:**

1) Describe how you perceive the interactions between yourself and the target pupil
in positive as well as negative terms

2) Describe how other staff perceive the target pupil
in positive as well as negative terms

3) Describe how you perceive the interactions between the target pupil and other pupils
in positive as well as negative terms

4) Describe how you perceive the interactions within the target pupil's family and between the family and the school

Designed by Don Clarke and Harry Ayers In '*Perspectives on Behaviour*' Published by David Fulton

5) Describe any comparisons you are able to make between any observations undertaken of the target pupil: does this comparison highlight discrepencies or agreements. If so, what implications does it have for your picture of the pupil?

6) From the above information, summarise your perceptions and those of others and state your expectations of the target pupil.

7) If possible, REFRAME those perceptions in such a way that the target pupil's problem is redefined more positively. Describe your 'reframing'.

PUPIL SELF-CONTROL MONITORING FORM

Name:

Date:

Form / Class:

Underline appropriate words or phrases and add any others that seem relevant

1) Where did the incident take place?

Class	Toilets	Corridor
Playground	Trip	Stairs
Dining Hall	To or from school	Gym
Assembly	Other	

2) What took place?

A pupil teased me	A teacher told me off	A pupil cussed me
A pupil took my things	A pupil annoyed me	A pupil hit me
I did something wrong	Other	

3) Who was involved?

A friend	Another pupil	An adult
Other		

4) What did you do?

Hit back	Told a teacher	Ran away
Told another adult	Shouted	Walked away calmly
Cried	Talked it through	Lost my temper
Broke something	Told a friend	Took no notice
Other		

5) How did you feel? I felt ..... I felt like .....

6) How upset did you get?

Extremely	Very	Mildly	A little	Not at all

7) How well did you control yourself?

Extremely	Very	Mildly	A little	Not at all

8) What could you do differently next time?

Designed by Don Clarke and Harry Ayers In '*Perspectives on Behaviour*' Published by David Fulton

COGNITIVE ASSESSMENT PUPIL QUESTIONNAIRE

This form can be used as a means of assessing a pupil's thoughts, attitudes, expectations and beliefs in the school context.

Circle appropriate number on each continuum and underline or add relevant words

Unless otherwise indicated: 1 = Poor 3 = OK 5 = Excellent

BEHAVIOUR:

What do you THINK about your behaviour in:

1) Classrooms	1	2	3	4	5	**2) Corridors**	1	2	3	4	5
3) Assembly	1	2	3	4	5	**4) Toilets**	1	2	3	4	5
5) Playground	1	2	3	4	5	**6) Outside school**	1	2	3	4	5

7) How do you generally behave? 1 2 3 4 5

Interfering Helpful Unhelpful Rude Polite Violent Friendly Talkative Loud Quiet Hardworking Lazy

8) What do you like about school?

9) What don't you like about school?

10) Which pupils do you like to play with?

10) Which pupils do you work with best?

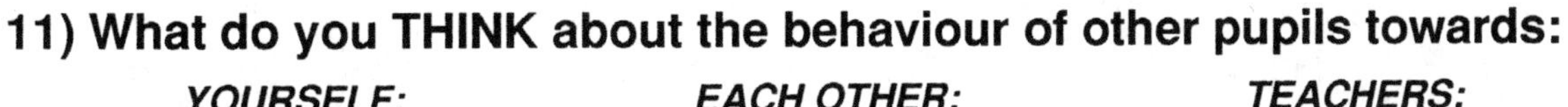

11) What do you THINK about the behaviour of other pupils towards:

YOURSELF: 1 2 3 4 5

EACH OTHER: 1 2 3 4 5

TEACHERS: 1 2 3 4 5

12) What do you think of your school? 1 2 3 4 5

Too small Just the right size Too big Poorly decorated Pleasantly decorated

Badly designed Too hot Too cold Badly lit Too noisy Too crowded

Designed by Don Clarke and Harry Ayers In '*Perspectives on Behaviour*' Published by David Fulton